# LOVING ME,
# LOVING YOU

**About the author:**

Brenda Schaeffer is author of the popular book *Is It Love or Is It Addiction?* and the four pamphlets in Hazelden's Healthy Relationship Series. A licensed psychologist and a certified transactional analyst, she lectures nationally and internationally. She is an experienced psychotherapist, trainer of therapists, lecturer, and communications consultant. She has trained with experts in hypnosis, Gestalt, bioenergetics, visual imagery, existential, transpersonal, regression, and developmental psychologies.

A Clinical and Provisional Teaching Member of the International Transactional Analysis Association, she is Director of Brenda M. Schaeffer and Associates in Minneapolis, where she conducts training, workshops, and therapy.

# LOVING ME, LOVING YOU

## Balancing Love and Power
## In a Codependent World

Brenda Schaeffer

■ HAZELDEN®

First published April 1991.

ISBN: 0-89486-747-4
Printed in the United States of America.
Library of Congress Catalog Card Number: 90-85023

Editor's note:
Hazelden Educational Materials offers a variety of information on chemical dependency and related areas. Our publications do not necessarily represent Hazelden's programs, nor do they officially speak for any Twelve Step organization.

The vignettes in this book are composites of actual situations and persons. The autobiographies are real, although the names have been changed. Other names and events have been created by the author for illustrative purposes. Any resemblance to specific persons, living or dead, or specific events, is entirely coincidental.

The following publishers have generously given permission to use extended quotations from copyrighted works:

From *The Ages of Gaia*, by James Lovelock. Copyright 1988 by W. W. Norton & Company, Inc. Reprinted with permission.

From *The Tangled Wing*, by Melvin Konner. Copyright 1983 by Henry Holt and Company, Inc. Reprinted with permission.

From *The Chalice and the Blade*, by Riane Eisler. Copyright 1988 by HarperCollins Publishers. Reprinted with permission.

From *The Prophet*, by Kahlil Gibran. Copyright 1969 by Alfred A. Knopf. Reprinted with permission.

# Contents

# Acknowledgments

The authoring of this book has been a spiritually transforming experience. I recognize I am different, having been honored with "its" task. I could not have known beforehand that each day would speak to me of the very theme I write about: balancing love and power.

I am deeply appreciative of the many relationships that provided nourishment, challenging feedback, and support throughout the process. In these relationships, I was reminded that we are not islands but profoundly connected, and that it is in this connectedness that miracles unfold and ideas become creations. I wish to thank Doug Toft for his sensitive editorial feedback and taking the time to truly know me; Sally Graham for her wonderful spirit and willingness to work odd hours to meet typing deadlines; and Hazelden editor Rebecca Post for respecting professional meanings behind my words and representing me so well to her colleagues. In addition, I want to thank Hazelden editors Jeff Petersen and Don Freeman for their work.

I appreciate those who took the time to read and objectively review the manuscript. Their feedback was invaluable: my brothers, Michael and Gregory Furtman; colleagues and spirited friends, Jan Gagne, Laura Gauger, Dr. Barton Knapp, Mary Klake, Pam Benson, Dr. Russell DesMarais, and Ted Harrison. Thanks is also due to Diana Pauling for lending her spiritual insight and guidance when it was needed.

I am deeply indebted to those who wrote their stories and those who did not write their stories and inspired me nevertheless. I am honored to know each of them and to be witness to their intimate journeys.

I must not forget those clients, students, and staff who, though they did not always like the time I took to write, encouraged and applauded me along the way. *Thank you!*

To Ted, and my children Heidi and Gordy—thank you for the heartfelt love and patience. You shared your spiritual lover when it was most needed. To my father Ralph Furtman—thank you for the caring reminders to sustain balance in my life.

# Introduction

*Here is a test to find whether your mission on earth is finished.*
*If you're alive, it isn't.*

*— Richard Bach*

A love relationship can be the most precious gift that we can experience in our lifetime. Yet, the amount of emotional, physical, spiritual, and mental battering that takes place in relationships is staggering. Witness the people in relationships who strike out, yell, ignore, ridicule, and call each other names—and, at the same time, profess to love. Battering is so pervasive that people question whether love really exists. This book affirms for the cynics that, indeed, healthy love exists. But its point is that a relationship is not a neat little package. A relationship is a living process that begins and ends with you.

## HEALTHY RELATIONSHIPS—A CONTINUING QUEST

Nothing in this book is new. Everything in it has been said or thought of before. Knowledge is simply there, like an electric current, ready to be tapped and expressed. Why, then, read further?

Because, like me, you are responding to an inner quest to affirm what some deeper part of you already knows and may not have words to say. Because, like me, you are called to a deeper level of living where action comes from the quiet place within. Because, like me, you have discovered that relationships compelled by desire, fear, and social obligations die or create an inner death to your authenticity. Because, like me, you long to resonate with that which is divine in life and in you. Because, like me, you are ready to take back control of your psyche from shaming authorities of the past and present. Because, like me, you are ready to step into the tradition of human bravery, to stop blaming others for who you are and face your fears with the conviction of a warrior. And because, like me, as you've claimed the inner knowing and acted on it, you have been criticized and abandoned by those who didn't understand.

Change that involves departure from the old and familiar produces fear. People committed to knowing the truth that sets them free are often seen as a threat, and they will feel pressure to resist change. Primitive cultures provided rites of passage to help its members deal with this fear and give dignity to the transition. However, our present day often seems void of meaningful rituals that support the perilous journey into the darkness of self. What's more, we often fail to see the depth of meaning our common rituals do offer—the rituals of baptisms, weddings, graduations, and funerals. One day we may return to powerful meanings in rituals. Until then, the stories of others can provide the hope and support lacking in everyday life.

Without such models to support our change, we often yield to the old and familiar. It can be hard to put ideals into practice, even when we feel certain of them: "Though the spirit is strong, the flesh is weak." Ultimately we must walk our path alone. Even so, who amongst us is not encouraged and supported by the heroic stories of those who also take a personal journey of change and growth? That's one need that this book, in part, can fill.

### The Hundred-Piece Puzzle

To get to know love, we must first realize that we are not who we think we are, and accept that we do not have all the answers. Life is like a hundred-piece puzzle, and we are lucky to get ten, twenty, even thirty of those pieces by the time we complete adolescence. We enter early adulthood with the illusion that we have what we need to live our lives successfully and form healthy relationships. Well intending, we thrust ourselves into life, believing we know who we are. We trust we have what is needed to be in the world and the confidence to do what we are meant to do.

It may not take long before we discover the betrayal. Some important pieces of life's puzzle are missing, and some that we do have are faulty. This often became most evident in our relationships. But at the same time, we're afraid to tell anyone we feel broken, fallen, or insecure, because if they have the hundred pieces to life's puzzle, they may conclude that something is wrong with us.

And so we join the world of great pretenders. We get caught up in a life of illusion: greed, possessions, pretension, compulsions, addictions, roles. We do whatever we can do to survive in the world, pulling ourselves up by our bootstraps and attempting to resemble something called "normal."

In our desperation, we attempt to make what is empty seem real. We control our lives through denial, rationalizations, comparisons, and power plays. We become entrenched in our illusion, demanding status and recognition, assessing people in terms of how useful they can be to us. We do things to "be somebody" or belong to someone. Egoism and ignorance prevail. Ill-informed, we might never know that our nobility is in what we can become and how we can love. Slowly we lose touch with our authentic spirit, our state of grace. Essence, the core of our individuality, sits silently, patiently waiting to be recognized.

If we fail to realize the loss of self (or illusionary nature), life, true to form, inevitably provides what we need: a major shock. That shock may be a divorce, a separation, the death of a loved one, a prolonged illness, or simply a sense of void. In any case, such events jolt us into recognizing that much of what we know is hollow, that life is out of balance.

The recognition that our life has been an illusion can be terrifying, for it demands we give up the old and familiar, that we leave our denial and take personal responsibility for life. We confront questions about the purpose and meaning of life that have gone previously unanswered. In our anxiety, we may cling to old addictions and destructive relationships, continuing to satisfy our hunger for predictability. Paradoxically, in such moments, we may enter an altered state of consciousness that can, if we let it, help us see what really matters. Once we get in touch with our urge to stay conscious and be all that we can be, we can reach out for help, for guidance—the missing puzzle pieces.

As a psychotherapist, I view such change as a sign of wellness, not sickness. A person who is honest enough to say, "I don't have all the puzzle pieces and I want more of my life, more love in my relationships," is wise, not sick.

## Relationships Are a Mirror

In such moments of real insight, we encounter a fundamental truth. Relationships are a matrix within which we either grow or wither. Nowhere but in a relationship do we encounter ourselves so directly and so clearly at our best and our worst. Nowhere but in relationships do we experience or inflict so much pain, suffering, and abuse. And nowhere but in love relationships do we experience such profound joy, ecstasy, and intimacy that connect us with all that is wondrous, that is bliss.

We long for mature love—a love that bonds us with others and yet allows us freedom. But frequently we fall short of our mark. Why? Often because our relationships harbor elements of unhealthy dependency that creep into the best of love relationships. Such dependency means that we look to someone outside ourselves—sometimes compulsively—to satisfy our yearning for security, sensation, power, identity, belonging, and purpose. This is *love addiction.*

The paradox is that love addiction is our attempt to maintain control. In so doing, however, we actually lose control by relinquishing personal power. And the cycle recurs, time and time again, like a worn record.

## LOVE CALLS US TO TRANSFORMATION

*Everything has to do with loving and not loving.*
— *Robert Bly*

The journey beyond love addiction or unhealthy love is a journey of personal transformation, one of profound magnitude. We must recognize that something in our conditioning has suppressed the spirit within, yet that spirit still exists. Our early human experiences with love and power successfully confused us and alienated us from our authentic self. This is the self who understands the real meaning of love and power: Love without power goes idle, yet power without love is intolerable. In short, love and power have been out of balance. It is imperative that out of the imbalance, power and love emerge as coauthors of life, beginning within you.

Much has been written about love, power, and personal transformation in and of themselves. What I'm about to share with you are some ideas that speak to their interrelatedness and may provide a helpful structure for your personal journey. My underlying premise is that life events, including pain in our love life, can be an opportunity to spiritually transform ourselves so we can know a deeper level of love and power. This book is the synthesis of many theories and schools, ideas and personal experiences. I have been influenced by Dr. Eric Berne, particularly his theory on life script and game analysis; by the widely known poet Robert Bly; and by the late Joseph Campbell, who focused on ritual and myths.

Many references to both Western and Eastern spiritual schools are included. I am also excited about what's happening in modern physics and how relationships can be viewed in the context of fundamental laws.

My belief is that love calls us to a state of wakefulness where we experience a freshness of spirit and freedom from a polluted mind. This calls for a grounding in our own goodness. If we want love, if we want to help the world, we have to take this personal journey. It is up to each of us to experience our own meaning and take that meaning into all of our relationships.

The first step is to break out of the persona created by our psychological development and discover the self we've learned to hide. The possibilities of self-knowledge go beyond our wildest imagination. But discovering that dimension cannot begin until we acknowledge that we are asleep and that only occasionally do we escape from our constricted self-images. No one, including me, likes to hear this. And yet, it is here that we can start to learn the most powerful lessons about love.

The goal is to become a more loving and powerfully conscious person. This is not easy. We must first learn about our selves—what we became, what we can become, and how this duality affects our spirit.

A book is a teacher—one who reminds you of what it is you already know. It is my challenge to put the news in a paradigm that helps you connect with what is there waiting to be stirred up, kindled, owned, made manifest. My hope is that what I am about to share stirs something in you.

## WHY I WROTE THIS BOOK

This book is a sequel to my book *Is It Love or Is It Addiction?* Several events inspire me to write again. One was a question my son asked in his adolescence: "What is the reason most people seek your help?" I began reflecting on the stories of my clients and on the literature of my profession. The number one problem could be summed up in one phrase: i*dentity crisis.* Most people go through life not knowing who they really are, only who they have learned to become.

This reminds me of a Taoist saying: "The real is empty, the empty is real." That is, the self we learned to become is hollow. It consists mainly of adaptations we made early in life to get our needs met, to cover up the lack of love, the emptiness we might have felt inside—the void. Addictions, compulsive behaviors, and even therapy can be a frantic attempt to fill that void. And yet the void is real. That inner sense of emptiness and despair is the real self calling us back home. We can face that void, even befriend it, and come out whole on the other side.

The greatest challenge we face is letting go of the life of illusion as we've come to know it. As the late Joseph Campbell wrote in *The Hero with a Thousand Faces*, all heros must go through a psychological death. They must first die to the infantile impressions of the ego and experience a resurrection that transcends ordinary consciousness. To grow up is to wake up and acknowledge that we have been put to sleep by our conditioning. My son's question blatantly reminded me that the problem of identity was the developmental challenge and task of my adolescent son. Normal development assumes that by young adulthood I know, love, and trust myself, and have power within me to live life with others in an honoring way. How many of us have really attained this? Is it possible that many of us have been developmentally arrested in adolescence? So my first reason for writing this book is to help people know who they really are, to transcend who they have learned to become.

A second reason is to provide information to the growing number of men and women who quest for healthier love relationships. I'm deeply concerned about what is happening in our culture between men and women. We have loudly proclaimed liberation for both men and women for well over two decades. Yet, men and women continue to be at war with each other. They blame each other for the ills in relationships and society. The life stories of men and women tell us that love addiction, or unhealthy dependency on others, is not gender selective. Yet, many men and women still lack understanding and tolerance of each other. How is it that men can be raised to become the very thing women hate? How and why can women be raised to become what men need and yet fear—a fear they dare not admit to? And why do the masculine and feminine principles in each person so easily become unbalanced? These questions need answering.

My third reason for writing this book is to clarify the delicate relationship between love and power. I recall a scene in my childhood when at age five I approached an elderly neighbor couple to sell a church raffle ticket. The husband bought one, and as he began writing his name, his wife grabbed the pen and reproached him: "You don't know how to write your name. Give me that pen!"

As a child, my soul hurt so deeply at this misuse of power that I excused myself and found a quiet place to cry. I could not understand how people who claimed to love each other could hurt each other so deeply. I looked around and saw other grown-ups hurt each other too. I felt confused, and I believe that most children in the world have experienced some of that confusion when it comes to the concept of love.

I recognized even then, as I do now, that the way people express love has something to do with their beliefs about power—their capacity to produce change. When love is without power, we take care of others at our own emotional expense. When power is without love, we abuse, hurt, and injure others—ultimately at our own expense. Our task, then, is to build affirming relationships—the peak experience of all peak experiences—where love and power are in balance.

## WHAT THIS BOOK IS ABOUT

The premise of this book is that a basic wisdom or way of experiencing the world is always available to us, one that can guide us to more loving relationships. That way of seeing can be called our *spiritual lover*. When we learn to live from our spiritual lover, we discover how to balance love and power in our relationships. In balance we relate, resolve conflict, and solve problems with compassion, intuitive insight, and caring that transcend our ordinary state.

Reaching our spiritual lover calls us to a path that may transform our lives. Mapping some of the high points on that path is the subject of this book.

*Indeed, even unhealthy love and other addictions can be viewed as a window to the soul.* For in addiction, some aspect in us knows that we are more than our experience, that we are more than who we think we are. We reach out for momentary relief, euphoria, or altered states of consciousness often kept at bay because of conditioning that has deadened or limited our spirit. We desire to go home to a place of peace and love. True, the "high" we feel in addiction is only a dim reflection of that place. But the place is real.

There is a saying, Ignorance is bliss. Ignorance is not bliss; ignorance is ignorance; bliss is something else. Bliss is bliss. There's a world of knowledge for us to tap into, but some of the knowledge has been carefully kept from us in many subtle ways. To know more bliss is to become knowledgeable, to see the broader picture. In reality, our addictions become misguided attempts to find our bliss. Addictions are a dead-end road in our journey, even though the journey is valid. In the words of American poet Robert Bly, the alcoholic is looking for spirit and finds the wrong one.

Our level of consciousness has a great impact on our relationships. "Level of consciousness" is a phrase that refers to which self is active in a person at any given moment. To think that we may have more than one self defies common sense. And yet consider the many selves we bring to any relationship. There's the angry self and the patient self, the strong self and the weak self. We have a self who asks another person to help us stop hurting, to fill a void in our life. Then there's the self who asks nothing at all from the other person, the self who simply celebrates the existence of another.

All these selves—and many more—exist in us. This book specifically talks about three selves and three different kinds of lovers that can come to life inside us. I call the three selves the *learned self*, the *autonomous self*, and the *spiritual self*. Often the learned self, operating from a life script, yields one kind of lover; I call it *addictive lover*. The autonomous self, free of addiction, naturally expresses another kind of lover: the *healthy lover*. Both of these selves are transcended in love by the spiritual self, which I call the *spiritual lover*.

We can visualize the relationship between each of these three selves and three lovers as follows:

```
Learned Self <————> Addictive Lover
Autonomous Self <————> Healthy Lover
Spiritual Self <————> Spiritual lover
```

This book, in essence, explains how these aspects of ourselves operate in our lives. Chapter One previews the main themes of the book, especially the processes of love, power, and transformation. In Chapter Two, we examine how love and power, the masculine and feminine principles in our relationships, have fallen out of balance. Chapters Three and Four focus on the three selves in more detail, while Chapter Five fleshes out the concept of the spiritual lover. Chapter Six focuses on principles, laws, and stages that guide the transformation of our love relationships. Chapters Seven and Eight return to a discussion of love and power in light of what we've learned about the spiritual lover. Chapter Nine explores how spiritual love draws us beyond ourselves and into the world.

Equally important, however, is the crucible of experience, the events and emotions that shape your life. The most powerful teaching comes about when ideas *and* experience are combined. In this book you'll encounter many ideas. Some may be new, while others are already familiar to you. In either case, I encourage you to absorb these ideas, add your experiences, and use this knowledge in a way that can really make a difference in your daily life. Optional self-help activities are included throughout this book to help you apply these ideas in your life. Many of the exercises in the Activities sections in this book were designed to be used in workshops and in therapy. They were designed not to be completed hurriedly. The time and thought you put into them can help you grow into a self-awareness process. These exercises are usually done with professional guidance. In the event that you find them difficult to do on your own or if doing them elicits discomfort, seek professional help. Though their purpose is serious, they are designed to be fun and insightful.

## MY STORY

The crucible of experience is one of our most important teachers, and this includes even the most painful experiences. For it is here that we receive some of the most powerful lessons about relationships. To make this clear, I offer one chapter in my own story.

It's a story that started my personal transformation—the death of my mother. The story is a deeply personal one, and a part of me hesitates to share that which is so personal. It's risky, for I share a view of my mother's life and death that may be different than how my relatives may view it. But that is how it should be.

I knew my mother well. I watched her every day of my life, much more closely than she or I imagined. She was a gentle, loving spirit, childlike at times, and deeply sensitive to others' pain. She never injured anyone.

My mother had one flaw as I saw it: insecurity. She didn't fully feel or believe in her worth and personal power. My mother was orphaned at age two. By that I mean, though she always had her mother nearby, she never knew her real father. She lived in an orphanage with her sister for a while. Her mother worked there until she found an older man to marry and take care of them all. And so, as far back as I can remember, I became my mother's keeper. I wanted her to be happy even at my own expense. Part of my life plan, my conditioning, became to care for others and forget about my needs. In addition, I know now that part of my giving to my mother was spiritual love.

I recall having a deep spiritual connection with my mother then, but I knew that I couldn't give her what her mother and father failed to give. Yet in my grandiosity, I thought that if I loved her as much as she loved me, maybe she'd know how wonderful she was and find her bliss.

When she was near age fifty, my mother had an aneurysm [a cerebral hemorrhage]. I had been with her only the day before, and both of us had known something was about to happen. She wanted to sit by me, touch me, walk with me into nature. As we walked, she looked at things with that final look of intimacy, taking everything in as though she was saying farewell. As we parted, she kissed and hugged me, looked me in the eyes and said her final good-bye.

While I was driving back home to another city, a bird flew into the window of my car and died. I immediately thought of my mother and looked at my watch. The phone was ringing as I unlocked the door of my house. My mother had severe cerebral bleeding and was not expected to live. She was in the ambulance at the same time the messenger, the bird, hit my window.

My mother remained in a coma, her life supported only by machines. It wasn't long before she was pronounced brain dead and the life systems were scheduled to be removed. My father wished for her not to be alone, yet he was too distressed to be with her. My three brothers and sister preferred not to be there either. But I was my mother's keeper, and so I agreed.

I don't know if you've ever watched someone close to you go from life to death. It was both horrific and awe inspiring. I watched my mother's body go from white to ashen to gray, then to a purplish black. I knew when her spirit left; it was there in the room with me.

Something significant happened to me in that moment of chaos. I was catapulted into an altered state of consciousness where I saw life clearly, and I knew that there was an important message in the awfulness of the experience. It was a peak experience, telling me something about the nature of who I was in relationship to all of life. For a few moments I felt a profound connection to everything. I knew what really mattered and didn't matter. I told myself not to forget the importance of this moment, the death of my mother.

In that moment, images of history flashed before me, most clearly that of my maternal heritage, the models for my womanhood. My great-grandmother died near age fifty; my grandmother died in spirit near age fifty; my mother's only sibling, her sister, preceded her in death near age fifty; and here I was witness to my mother dying at near age fifty.

In that moment something in me stirred. Something shifted. I experienced that moment where stillness and movement meet. I was never the same again. Perhaps it was what's been called an opening of the heart. At any rate, a profound religious experience occurred. I didn't need a faith; I was experiencing faith. In my mother's death, I was more fully alive than I had ever been. I was awake. *All at once, a sense of love merged with power and knowing.* I made a promise to myself, my mother as my witness: This loving without power will not happen to me.

I didn't understand fully what the promise meant or where it would take me, but I knew it was right. There was something in my mother's dying that gave me permission to live my life fully. I also knew the promise was not about whether I lived beyond near fifty. It was about freedom to be me. The ability to know a much deeper meaning of love and power, to take the depth of love, power, and knowing of the moment and translate it into everyday, ordinary experience.

As I witnessed the lives of my women ancestors, I recognized that they represented some of the best aspects of the feminine principle: love, nurturance, openness, receptivity, earth. Yet, they did not have full understanding of personal power. They empowered others, especially men. They also looked constantly to their children. I saw how in their lives, love without personal power didn't make it.

I walked back into my life in a state of shock that still allowed me time to grieve, to say good-bye to my mother, and to support my father. I knew in that moment that I had an urgent need to experience all aspects of myself. I began experiencing things differently. Living as I had been, the spirit in me would die. With that knowledge I began making more choices from the inner life, the real me, frightening as that was. I began discarding that which no longer felt genuine or real. I no longer needed an Academy Award for acting.

I felt shaky and scared in this quest for my true identity. I had no idea where in the world I was going. It was so much easier being told what to be and where to go and how to get there. I was leaving all that was comfortable, safe, predictable. Some people didn't like me anymore. Through it all I grieved, I despaired, I was punished. I felt pulled toward both the old and the new and danced back and forth between them. Often I resorted to old, familiar ways to feel safe. I had no models and I felt very alone. Even so, I said to myself: *Just follow your heart, that inner knowing. Remember, you did it as a child. You know how.* That inner knowing became my salvation.

And so I struggled, I fell, and I climbed. I laughed joyously and I wept. I was abandoned, terrified that I had made the wrong choice. Many times there were doubts: How do I know I can trust what I'm experiencing? How do I know God exists? How do I know I might not fall and never get up? Somehow, though, I knew it was important to experience fully every step of the way: the terror, the aloneness, the suffering, the grief, the doubt, the rage, the self-questioning. Something inside me said: *Keep following yourself.* It was truly an act of faith.

Faith, hope, the love of others almost gone, I began coming out of my darkness. I read voraciously and looked for encouragement everywhere. I began understanding the meaning of the sentence, "You have to die in order to be reborn." I had to die to the old and the familiar, the illusions of my conditioning. And there were times I longed to be unconscious again, asleep. This trip I was on felt too difficult and lonely. I learned that once a person begins seeing life in Technicolor, it's impossible to view it in black and white again. There is no turning back unless we are willing to live a lie.

That brings me to where I am today. I can truthfully say that my life has been a most incredible journey. The depth of pain, suffering, and despair has offered me the gift of joy, ecstasy, and bliss. It helped me realize how banal I had become, how ordinary. I now look back at the choices I made from my intuitive wisdom, choices that seemed totally disconnected from logic. Those choices were exactly what was needed to bring me to the next step. There have been so many days I've said, "Thank God I had the courage to listen to myself, even when terrified and uncertain."

Initially I grabbed on to faith, to support systems, to affirm I was doing it right. Now I believe I've found my center and most times live from it. I am more at peace than I've ever been. I more often experience life with a sense of wonderment. I am more connected with all aspects of life, more concerned about the earth and my relationship to it. Perhaps most important, I'm willing to acknowledge when I'm off course, when I'm being real and when I'm not.

The relationships I have in my life are deep and enriching. I have abundance, I'm living my meaning. Frankly, I'm amazed at all I've experienced and completed since my mother's death. It far surpasses my wildest imagination.

I have a son and daughter whom I deeply respect and am glad to call my friends. I have friends who are committed to their personal journeys and who follow their own spiritual paths. The work I do on myself benefits them as well, for it transforms all my relationships. I even envision my mother, my aunt, my grandmother, and my great-grandmother applauding me—not because I need their applause, but because I free them too.

Giving thanks, I reflect now on the experience of my mother's untimely death as her gift to me. Even if it wasn't her intent to give me a gift, I have made it one. I am grateful that I accepted the gift of freedom. I am closer to the meaning of love, power, and personal transformation. I understand that *conscious living is a process*. It is intimacy with myself, being who I am and becoming who I can become at the same time.

As I listen to myself and create my experience, I continually become more of who I already am. When I connect with others and the universe at that level, I experience a profound intimacy that says, *This is it. This is life. This is God*. And when I'm there, it all seems so simple. My human self, like yours, knows how much pain, suffering, and conditioning must be transcended to experience these moments. And it is in the midst of our pain that, if we are willing, we can come to a transformed understanding of love and power.

## CHAPTER ONE

# Love, Power, And Transformation

*Every man on this planet is taking his initiation in love.*
*— Florence Scovel Shinn*

Sometimes, only half-jokingly, people have said, "God, give me patience—and make it now." We can probably identify with that need to have things made better—now. To be free of pain—now. To rediscover our capacity for love—now.

Even when our brain tells us that change is an ongoing process, we often rage against that knowledge. We want to know the answers immediately, and we want those answers to magically transform our life into the complete, meaningful entity it was meant to be—now. This urgency for positive outcomes is often translated into a frenzied search through self-help books, seminars, and group participation.

Clearly, in our love relationships this urgency is apparent. Many of us have become disappointed when we discover that, despite our newly found knowledge, our love lives have changed little or not at all. That is because we become so preoccupied with procedure and end results that we fail to experience fully each moment of a relationship. We fail to see how that moment connects to the picture as a whole. We miss the evolutionary nature of the process. You are in this process, probably without even realizing it. The process' beauty and appeal is that it can give what most of us want more than anything: immediacy, for it is happening right now.

## SEEKING THE MEANING OF LOVE

Love is here to stay and, as you've learned, sometimes it feels good and sometimes it feels bad. Love's story is centuries old and the themes seldom change. Love is pain or yearning. Love is inspiration and awe inspiring. Love is ebb and flow.

One dictionary's definition says it well. "Love: A strong complex emotion or feeling causing one to appreciate, delight in, and crave the presence or possession of another; to please or promote the welfare of the other; devoted affection or attachment; the yearning or out going of the soul toward something that is regarded as excellent, beautiful or desirable."

In this one definition we find addictive love, healthy love, and spiritual love. No wonder we are so confused. We've been lead to believe they are all the same. Compulsive needing to possess another person is addictive love; promoting the welfare of another is healthy love; and the soul's reaching out is spiritual love. If a dictionary does not distinguish between the different kinds of love, be kind to yourself when you feel confused.

Love addiction began a long time ago and creeps into the best of relationships. Our relationships harbor elements of love addiction when we look outside ourselves to meet an unmet need, when we become more concerned about how we are loved than how to love. Love addiction detracts from our emotional, mental, spiritual, and physical well-being. The paramount feature is being out of balance in some way. We learn to take care of other people and deny parts of ourselves to survive.

Well, we did survive! And now we can let go of the past and our fears, heal the wounds, and get on with growing in healthy love. Real love is an energy that is seeking expansion. Real love, a natural state of being, is nourishing and healing by its very presence. Although we say it is something to be learned, in actuality it is something to be rediscovered. And there is much learning as we rediscover it.

### Is Dependency Always Bad?

With all that's been written and said about codependency and addiction, the word *love* often stimulates fear—so much so that legitimate dependency needs go unattended or are denied altogether. A client was describing his great emotional pain, and I asked him to reach out to his group members during this crisis. He panicked and quickly said, "I can't do that. That means I'm love addicted. I've got to take care of the pain myself." I asked him what would happen if he didn't reach out. "I'm afraid to think about it," he responded. "I've been doing that solo number for years, and I'm getting mentally and physically exhausted."

I could understand his double bind. In his letting go of a longstanding addictive relationship, he was fearful of creating unhealthy dependency again. He could not yet distinguish between addictive love and healthy love. He is not alone. Most struggle with the same dilemma.

Is dependency always bad? No, not at all. To understand relationships as a living process, it is important to identify three kinds of lovers in each of us: addictive, healthy, and spiritual.

## THE ADDICTIVE LOVER

*Addictive love* refers to taking care of other people at our emotional expense. It is a manipulative way to create dependence even when it is not needed. We deny parts of ourselves to keep people who meet our needs around. Addictive love is unhealthy because it is based on fear, control, illusions, and because it limits our growth. Our requests for help are indirect, manipulative, or evasive. We may even pretend we do not have needs. We may tough it out and pull ourselves up by our own bootstraps.

Addictive love results from inadequate loving, past or present. Our needs are legitimate, and our real self has always known that. As children, we did our part: When we felt discomfort, we identified the need and reached out for help. If we got no response, an inadequate response, or a negative one, we had no choice but to figure out another way to be taken care of.

When we don't get the response we need in our quest for love, we do the second best and form addictive attachments. However, even addictive love is useful as a temporary way of relating while we are learning to love ourselves, to trust ourselves, to work through the fears that keep us from reaching out in direct ways, and while developing tools for healthy love. Yet addictive love should only be temporary. Rather than being mutually beneficial, it is parasitic, for, like any parasite, it constricts and depletes.

### Relationship Dependency Is Not Love Addiction

One point is crucial: Relationship dependency is not the same as addictive love. In fact, dependency can be a healthy part of any relationship. There are three kinds of dependency: primary dependency, addictive dependency, and interdependency.

*Primary dependency* refers to those times when we "borrow" parts of another's ego for specific needs and for a limited time. When we were children, we needed our parents and other adults to nurture, protect, and inform us until we could do the same for ourselves. This is primary dependency. This type of dependency is also positive in adult relationships when it supports our health and growth, when it is asked for directly, and when it assists someone in need. It is not okay when it is assumed or expected; when it stunts growth or governs a relationship.

*Addictive dependency* refers to taking care of other people at our emotional expense. We deny parts of ourselves to keep other people around us, hoping those other people will stay and meet our needs. Addictive dependency is unhealthy when it is based on fear and control and limits our growth. However, addictive dependency can be temporarily useful while we are learning to love ourselves, work through our fears, and develop the emotional tools to love.

*Interdependency* involves two adults in an atmosphere of openness and trust; they have equal power in the relationship, individual identities, and self-love. Though interdependency is always healthy, it is often hard to sustain for long periods of time because of our human needs. Therefore, healthy love must alternate between primary dependency and interdependency.

### What the Learned Self Is Like

Our unmet needs and deepest patterns bring us to the heart of the learned self. The learned self is adaptive, the part of you that joins in with the crowd, right or wrong. Adaptation is the process through which any life form adjusts to the world. Both physical and behavioral changes result from adaptation. For example, when we begin running for exercise, our body changes and our attitude toward pain changes as well.

The learned self is the part of you that G. I. Gurdjieff, the modern spiritual master, referred to as "asleep," the "machine" that believes it is awake simply because it is talking and doing and thinking and feeling. This self lives a life of illusion. It is easily influenced, compulsive, habitual, and addictive. In the words of P. D. Ouspensky, one of Gurdjieff's students:

> Man is a machine. All his deeds, actions, words, thoughts, feelings, convictions, opinions, and habits are the results of external influences, external impressions. Out of himself a man cannot produce a single thought, a single action. Everything he says, does, thinks, feels—all this [just] happens. Man cannot discover anything, invent anything. It all happens.[1]

The learned self analyzes, intellectualizes, denies. It can be macho, passive, and dependent. Only rarely will it accept deep wounds, and it will use power plays to sustain denial. This self can be love addicted, so enmeshed in the lives of others that it has forgotten who it is. It loves to be loved. Its growth is stunted, it is incomplete, it resists change, it thinks only in absolute and concrete terms. For example, fairy tales are understood at the most literal level: Cinderella becomes the victim looking outside herself for the answers to happiness. Jack, in the children's story about the gigantic bean stalk, becomes the man who never disobeys mother. The learned self is often grandiose and controls with power plays.

When we function from the learned self, we rarely experience anyone as equal. We are comparing, worrying, doubting. The learned self defines itself from the outside in. It can be hollow, shallow, and ego-driven.

This is the self that can get caught up in mechanical thinking, mind over matter, mind over spirit, in controlling the earth. Competitive social structures are an extension of the learned self. Above all, the learned self is a product of its life script—the plan it designs under the influence of others.

*Life Scripts—The Drama We Live*

Every life experience that you and I have had is recorded in the neurology of our body. Even so, we know only a small part of who we are. It has been said that we are lucky to recall one out of one thousand of those recorded experiences. Yet, the composite of our life experiences deeply influence

- who we think we are,
- the thoughts we have and don't have,
- the feelings we're free to express or not express,
- the actions we take and don't take, and
- the people we select in our partnerships.

That composite runs our show, even when we're unaware of this fact.

Our human nature, then, unconsciously lives out a life drama that has a beginning, a middle, and a predictable end. In Transactional Analysis, this drama is referred to as the life script. Some spiritual schools refer to it as the life of illusion. The life script is intended to help us survive in the limited world we knew. It serves a useful purpose, providing protection, security, and nurturance. The paradox is this: The script that protected us in childhood continues into adulthood and begins creating binds that prevent us from maturing.

There is a theory called the "100 percent intent ratio," which says that we have in our life what we intend to have. What we don't have we never intended, psychologically speaking. We each have a frame of reference, that composite of our total life experiences, through which we view the world. We often act as if that frame of reference is the only reality, and we make our most important life decisions from that often contaminated view. This is our life script, the essence of the learned self.

## THE HEALTHY LOVER

*Healthy love* is the kind of relationship where interdependency and support prevail. Again, this means that two adults with equal personal power, individual identities, and healthy egos relate in an atmosphere of openness and trust.

Ideally, growing up would allow us to experience a healthy love that meets our needs and affirms our right to be, feel, think, and do. Then, by around age eighteen, we would have a healthy identity. We would know, love, and trust ourselves. We would have a confidence that allows us to willingly reach out, easily take in, and readily let go. If this were our experience, we would go out into the world and relate to the other complete humans. These autonomous relationships would allow high levels of trust, intimacy, and spontaneity. We would share our wisdom and effectively solve problems. We would treat each other with respect, sharing love, affection, and power. Each time two people met, there would be a "we," a sense of relationship more expansive than the "I" and the "you" that come together as separate selves.

To achieve healthy love, we must understand that we are chained by our conditioning and faulty parenting. Then we must be willing to leave the past. No easy task. For though we may physically leave an addictive relationship, emotionally we can remain attached, as our fears and resentments attest. Leaving the past requires full ownership of the past and even reexperiencing it for a time. Dorothy expressed it this way:

**Dorothy's Story:** *"I've invested too much effort to let the old me get away with her tricks."*

> I recently ended a relationship with my boyfriend, Rich. It was difficult to do as I cared for him and was really "hooked in." It was one of the most powerful addictions I have experienced in relationships, and yet, my rewards with Rich or my goodies were zero—none. Yet until recently I stayed with him.

One day Rich called. I hadn't heard from him in about seven weeks. He had picked up a briefcase of mine we had talked about months ago, and he wanted to bring it over. My first instinct was, *Oh wow. Maybe he really does love me and it can work.* He wanted to stop by in an hour. I panicked and thought, *How can I take a shower, clean the house, find the right outfit, go to the tanning booth, have my makeup and hair perfect, brush the dog, and be ready for him in an hour?*

Another part of me said, *Wait! You don't have time. You are not mentally and emotionally ready for this. Who cares if your house is messy, and why, for heaven sakes, do you have to rush around and accommodate his schedule? The briefcase has been on hold for months!*

I began recognizing the hooks, the invitations. My addictive lover was still caring and wanting to see him for whatever reason. So I told him, "No, tomorrow is a better day. Thank you for getting it for me." And I felt much better about this decision. I allowed myself preparation time.

I can take time to see this for what it really is and not go backward. Maybe down the road I will find a nice friend in this man I care about but cannot be with now in an intimate relationship.

I'm new at my changes and I like the real me. I've invested too much effort to let the old me get away with her tricks. I've learned it's much lonelier in a bad relationship than being lonely alone!

## THE SPIRITUAL LOVER

Living from a stance of healthy love is one of the greatest gifts we can receive. Yet even more is possible for us. We can bring another lover—the spiritual lover—into our lives. Spiritual lovers are spiritual journeyers. Spiritual lovers are always co-creating with all of life.

Life and loving can be viewed as a journey of personal transformation. The transformation model proposes that we have two natures: a human nature and a spiritual nature.

The *human nature* is a biological entity, a body that has basic survival needs that must be met or it will die. Like other animals, humans will adapt to their environments in order to get those needs met. Many of these adaptations are necessary and useful, allowing for continued growth: We stop at red lights. We get to appointments on time. We eat the right foods.

Other adaptations, however, are unnecessary and can create psychological harm. When children are harshly scolded for being angry, they may stop expressing anger. Children who are pushed aside as they reach for affection may learn to limit their closeness to others. The human nature, responding to its urge to survive, intuitively perceives the environment and begins limiting the amount of autonomy, creative expression, and intimacy in exchange for the predictable and acceptable.

In this conditioning, we lose contact with our autonomous selves as negative conclusions, decisions, and beliefs get locked in our mind and begin directing our life: *I don't belong. It's not safe to be close. I'm bad.* By age eighteen, we have two distinct selves. One is who we were born to be, the autonomous self who knows *I belong,* that *closeness can be safe* and that *I am good.* This self becomes subservient to who we have become, the learned self.

The *spiritual nature,* by contrast, is that aspect of self that is wise, compassionate, truth-oriented. It may or may not have a religion; one need not believe in formal religion to be spiritual. The spiritual self houses the essence that is the seat of our hope, our intuitive wisdom, our prophetic visions, our spiritual yearnings. The spiritual lover cares with detachment. It makes choices without being judgmental. It responds to the urge to be and become all that it can be and to give its uniqueness to life. It seeks unity with a higher consciousness. It reaches for divine perfection, bliss, wonder, and mystical experiences. It is at one with the mysteries of life. *And, paradoxically, the spiritual lover requires a strong and integrated human personality to express itself.*

An important step in most, if not all, sacred schools is seeing our mechanical nature and the conflicting selves that lie within us. This requires unifying our addictive, healthy, and spiritual lovers. Without this synthesis our energies are scattered, blocked. The result is illness within ourselves and our relationships with others.

The core message of this book is that any problem, including those related to love and power, can be an awakening to our spiritual nature. And with this process comes the potential to transform our relationships, to move from addiction to healthy love and beyond—to our spiritual lover.

And why is transforming our relationships so important? Because our relationships are the foundations of our families, our families are the foundation of our communities, our communities are the foundation of our culture, and cultures are the foundation of our world. If we are ever to know harmony in the world, we must first know it in our love lives. We must co-create life with other spiritual lovers.

Problems in relationships cannot always be resolved. They must be outgrown or transcended. A spiritual lover can do this. It is only the spiritual lover who can heal the injuries. Spiritual lovers have a sense of humor that can lighten the heaviness. They display the cosmic sense of humor of Yoda, the character from Star Wars, who says, "My dear, my dear, you're not getting it. It's do or not do, and you're not doing it."

To have a spiritual lover means I experience the divine in you. It's not God out there and me here; it's not God doing our relationships. Instead, spiritual love is experiencing the God in us, the spiritual lover who's willing to resolve and clean up the messes. The spiritual lover is that part of us that lives love and life fully, passionately. It is active, alive, imaginative, creative, and aware.

## ALL THREE LOVERS ARE INSIDE US

A mature understanding of love recognizes how we move in and out of all three lovers. For example, moving from the addictive lover to the healthy lover calls for effort, for support networks, or primary dependency as previously described. Our learned self has been so conditioned and injured that we cannot grow in love of self and others or change long-standing behavior patterns and beliefs without support. This is what AA (Alcoholics Anonymous), Al-Anon, ACA (Adult Children of Alcoholics), therapy groups, and support communities of any kind are about. And, to be effective, our support systems must be going the same direction we are.

We bring into our relationships all three kinds of love. Sometimes it's difficult to distinguish which is which, as Margie points out.

*Margie's Story: All Three Lovers Activated at Once*

> A friend called me with some disappointing news. I felt all three lovers activate at once. My addictive lover felt scared and wanted to mask it with anger and hang up; my healthy lover wanted to feel sadness and to reach out for information and reassurance; my spiritual lover wanted to express compassion in a way that considered both our needs.

It's important to recognize the differences between these lovers, to trust what feels right, to learn from what feels wrong. Tad, a workshop participant, said: "I never knew that my relationship had all three lovers, so when my relationship felt good, I tended to think of it as deception and made the good feeling go away. I knew my relationship was addictive and decided this good stuff can't be for real. It's a relief to know it is!"

Seeing the differences between the lovers inside us can help us resolve conflict, as Lynn's story reminds us. At one point she deeply pondered, *How can I remain in a relationship where my partner continues to close me out?* Her three lovers each had a point of view.

*Lynn's Story: Knowing the Difference Between the Three Lovers*

> ADDICTIVE LOVER: I'm ready to quit but I'm afraid to go. If I separate, it will be all over. I'll feel like a failure. The only thing I can do is push, pull, and make him open up and see his faults or hold out! I can threaten to leave.

> HEALTHY LOVER: I can tell him how I feel, what I need, how long I can wait, and let go. I can nurture his pain and acknowledge that he learned to be this way and he can change if he chooses. I can structure time and ways to resolve our differences. I can state clearly that I want to stay and that I know I'll also be okay alone. I can release my hurt and anger in straight ways. I can own the things I do that reinforce his closing me out.

SPIRITUAL LOVER: I am remembering the tremendous joy, innocence, and love that has become like a veiled statue and needs to be put into flesh and blood. I see his injuries and feel compassion. I can illuminate the way out of this mess. I definitely need to show more of me and stop getting so caught up in my pain and fear.

You can know the difference between these lovers too. Healthy love is your natural state of being. Spiritual love is your potential. Addictive love was learned, and it can be changed because it is not natural to you. You learned it after you got burned or betrayed. You can explore your past to discover when your trust was violated. But while you are there, remember: *The past, the present, and the future are all one. You are only looking at the past that is present in the now and interfering with the future.*

## THE ROLE OF POWER PLAYS

Power plays are manipulative behaviors aimed at keeping relationship partners in a one-up, one-down melodrama. Although instinctively intended to keep our lives safe, predictable, and in control, they don't. But, ironically, the excitement and drama of the power play can itself become addictive. Not surprisingly, manipulative behaviors are usually the most painful to confront.

Why the hesitancy to confront power plays? Fear. Fear that I might discover my own truth; fear that I must give up my denial; fear that I might discover I do indeed power play; fear that I might make contact with my feeling of powerlessness; fear that I might discover my relationship is addictive; fear of change, the unknown. For, indeed, when power plays are present, we can no longer deny our love is addictive.*

To have a healthy sense of personal power, I must know and love myself. I must believe I can live with others in an honorable way. When love is without power, our addictive lover emerges. We take

---

* If you're curious about how you may use power plays, a list of common power plays is included in an appendix at the back of this book, page 218.

care of others at our own emotional expense. When power is without love, we abuse and manipulate, ultimately at our own expense. That, too, is the addictive lover.

## Power Playing Is the Opposite of Power Sharing

Power plays emanate from the learned self that lives a life filled with greed, addictions, possessions, pretensions, roles, fear. That self thinks of power as a commodity that you are given by others, or as something that can be taken away. This is scarcity thinking: Somehow, there is not enough okay-ness, good feelings, and importance to go around.

You've no doubt heard or said these words: "I gave her my power." "He took my power away." "She overpowered me." "I'm giving back your power." Such statements are illusions. They define power as an item that can be given away and lost forever unless someone returns it or we steal it back and keep it under lock and key. The truth is, we act as though we gave our power away or took it from others. It is important to take responsibility for our actions. How different our lives would be if we said, "I acted as though I gave him my power." "She acted as though she took my power away." "I acted as though she overpowered me." These statements are freeing.

## "I" Versus "You" Ignores the Cohesive "We"

Often at the point when individuals or couples seek help with their relationships, they are so entangled that they have difficulty knowing where one person's boundaries stop and where the other's begin. This is a sign of confusion about power. Here the "I" has become "You," or the "You" has become "I." Or, the "I" wants you to become another "I" or "You" wants "I" to become yet another "You"—to think, feel, and act in familiar ways. And often, each person wants help in changing the other so he or she can be understood.

What continues to amaze me is how seldom the "I" and the "You" create or even discuss the "We." When two people get together, "I" assume "You" view the world the way "I" do (and vice versa), and if not, "You" should! Each has an image of a relationship from past experiences and believes the other person shares that image. Most "I dos" are said without ever having checked out the other's frame of reference. Frankly, it may be premature since "I" and "You" are generally unconscious when they first meet. Some people are even angered, shocked, and confused at the suggestion that they take time to know themselves in order to strengthen their relationships. So they often return to power plays instead of working on themselves.

*Sharing Love and Power*

Our early human experiences successfully confused us and alienated us from our authentic self, the self who understands the true meaning of love and power. *The power of love is the basis of our spiritual lover. The love of power is the basis of the addictive lover.* As the power of love is free to express itself, the love of power diminishes. If we find it difficult to live with ourselves lovingly and believe power is a commodity outside ourselves, then we cannot truly love or share power. And if we can't share love and power in our closest relationships, how in this world can we translate love and power to our community, our nation, and our planet?

## THE MEANING OF POWER

Had we received everything we needed in our development, we would have a healthy sense of identity, one allowing for us to share power in loving ways. *Power is our own personal potency, an energy that originates from within and reaches outward to meet our basic needs.* Power is the ability to produce change. For example, acid has the power to corrode metal. The sun has the power to melt snow. A polished surface has the power to reflect light. Like us, these things have both active and potential power. This means that power resides within and naturally creates change.

Power is neutral, neither good nor bad. The sun doesn't horde its power, nor can it stop from melting snow. As a living human being, I am energy. Some of that energy is bound and some of it is free. In that context, being alive is the expression of my power. And, in being alive, I can't help but effect change.

That is true in relationships as well. In agreeing to be in a relationship, I am sharing my power with another. I may have learned to act more or less powerful because I believed it would keep me safe. I may hide my power but it is always there; it does not go away.

## Spirituality and Power

One of the greatest gifts that has come out of recognizing addiction is the awareness of a whole new reality that many never dreamed existed: life viewed from a spiritual perspective. Many struggle with this as they encounter the First Step of Alcoholics Anonymous, an admission of powerlessness over an addiction: "We admitted we were powerless over alcohol—that our lives had become unmanageable." This Step in humility, a gentle acceptance of oneself, presents a paradox. As I own the powerlessness of my learned self, I am free to fully experience the spiritual energy that flows through me. This creative energy connects me to a universal consciousness, helping me see that I am more than my addictions. With this discovery, I can start anew in search of my true identity.

In spiritual terms, *power is the core truth that flows through me as I allow myself to be a channel of higher wisdom.* It defines me as a *warrior*— one who faces fear; one who courageously discovers and actualizes who I really am. This is the expression of my spiritual lover.

Some may wonder if this contradicts Step One, in which a person admits powerlessness over addictions. In reality, my spiritual lover supports that Step. Just as acid cannot stop from corroding metal, alcohol cannot stop from affecting the body. If we want to save the metal, we must remove it from the acid. If our lives are unmanageable because of a toxic relationship, we must change the properties of that relationship or remove ourselves. The slogan Let Go and Let God does not tell us to passively wait or deny our power. Rather it means power sharing with God as we understand God: changing what I can change, doing my part fully, then surrendering to universal laws and trusting in a positive outcome.

If you will, think of God as universal law. Letting go is power sharing with universal law. Control, or power playing, is running interference between self and universal law. If what you want is consistent with universal law, it will be there for you. If not, it cannot be.

## Power that Leads to Serenity

People who are comfortable with their power do not hurt others, nor do they need to prove they have power. Power can be a gentle firmness and directness. I think of Mohandas Gandhi, Mother Teresa, and Chief Joseph, the Native American spiritual leader. Each of these people lived his or her power. Their roles did not give them power nor define them. Instead, their roles were a natural expression of their identities, a means of expressing their power to effect change. In so doing, they gave evidence of a charisma and a relationship with the universe that transcends history. Many are threatened by such power. It often appears as though power players win, but whose legacy do we want to survive? The Adolf Hitlers or the Martin Luther Kings?

Power with a gentle firmness and directness can lead to a serenity that rises above even the fear of death. There is an ancient story about barbarians who invaded a village, killing all those who stood in their way. Entering a temple, one of these warriors met a humble monk who refused to flee. The warrior said, "Do you realize that without blinking an eye, I can kill you?" The monk replied, "Do you realize that without blinking an eye, I can be killed?"

## THE MEANING OF TRANSFORMATION

As I stated before, a key to healthy love is personal transformation. The most important relationship we have in our life is the one with ourselves. This is the one relationship we can count on for the rest of our life. It is essential to know what kind of a relationship I have with *me*.

Transformation requires facing my fears and conquering the self-doubt, negativity, and aggression that prevents me from loving fully. Doing so changes me so completely that I become another kind of being.

Transformation assumes that our human nature is one part of us and that the psyche contains the seed of our spiritual essence. It views *power* as the ability to create our own meaning in all that we do. Transformation calls us into using our body and mind to activate our spirit. As the Eastern spiritual schools explain, through transformation we can truly experience three aspects of our higher nature: truth, consciousness, and bliss.

Relationships can be viewed as an opportunity for this awakening. As such, transformation is far more than taking a pill to feel better, learning a technique to improve our sexual relationship, going through treatment, stopping an addiction, taking a mind control class, joining a support group, attending ACA, getting a divorce, or picketing for higher wages. Though these steps may well come first, transformation leads us beyond—to a serenity that no one can take away.

## PSYCHOLOGY AND RELIGION HAVE OFTEN FAILED US

Each spiritual school's intent has been for us to "know thyself," transcend our human conditioning, find our bliss, and release negative thinking that keeps us from abundance. Great permissions and directives, but frankly, for many years I had no idea how to do these things. Nor is it easy to find spiritual teachers who can tell us. And to complicate matters even further, psychology and religion, viewing human beings in totally different ways, each claimed to have the answer. We got lost in the shuffle.

It has been psychology's task to help us understand ourselves, to create a model of the huge store of influences that lie within us, and then to help free us from those limitations. For the most part, psychology has failed us. It continues to focus on the symptoms or to make the professional psychologist the keeper of the knowledge.

### Where Psychology and Sprituality Merge

Psychology as transformation challenges the orthodox assumptions of Western psychology; it blends East with West. Psychology viewed as transformation considers biology and the effects of conditioning. It still analyzes the impact of our life influences and acknowledges symptoms and relationship problems as important. It diagnoses, tests, even prescribes.

And yet psychology as transformation does far more. It considers process, energy, and holistic healing. It trusts intuition and it believes in loving the client. It considers spirit. It has a global view, recognizing that the health of each relationship, each society, and the earth itself depends on the harmonious interrelationship of psyche and spirit within each person. It is here where psychology and spirituality merge and where the seed of our truth lies dormant, waiting to be experienced.

## AWAKENING TO OUR ILLUSIONS

It is true, and sad, that we often don't realize how alienated we have become unless we are faced with some major life event that comes crashing in on us and says, Stop! Some people come to this knowledge all at once through life events that they do not ask for. War veterans, for example, encounter this, as do rape victims and people who have had near-death experiences. Denial may keep the lessons from these experiences at bay for a while only.

What these people experience is not a gift in any conventional sense. And yet, there is a gift in it for them if they want it: the opportunity to get real; the chance to contemplate the meaning of life and death; the chance to look at the quality of their relationships. The challenge, as always, is to do so in a world where most people believe they are choosing rather than reacting from a life plan that they previously created, a plan now recorded in their unconscious minds.

Others more slowly evolve into the awareness of illusion by the inner rumblings of discontent, or a vague sense of remembering a self long lost. This awareness is marked by chaos in your relationships, or by discovering that you are doing, feeling, or thinking things that you promised yourself you'd never do, feel, or think.

True to our learned self, we want a quick fix. While sometimes Band-Aid therapy can be performed, it is important to acknowledge the possibility of pain being related to something much deeper and more long lasting than previously thought. To have long-term relief, it is important to investigate the experience of our inner reality, and to examine how what happens to me makes perfect sense in terms of that reality. It is essential to understand more about the "what in me" that generates my experiences.

Sooner or later, all of us must confront our part in the messes in our relationships and decide how we can change in order to contribute to the greater whole. Each of us must examine our state of unconsciousness and see how that affects the relationships we draw into our life, the habitual patterns we are repeating. Seeing the big picture of how this happens is our task. This big picture contains not only our most immediate psychological influences, but years of historical references that contribute to the misunderstanding of love and power. Such is the theme of our next chapter.

## ACTIVITY

Every form of life has its own consciousness. It is important to understand this principle—we are who we are. Nature does not fight this. Nor does it worry about if we fit in or if we are good enough. It doesn't require plastic surgery. These aspects are seen only in people who have become self-conscious, critical, and removed from their true identity. The following exercise demonstrates these important aspects.

Nature is neutral. We cannot escape vulnerability. There are two forces—life and death—we must always deal with. We need both material and spiritual qualities to realize our fullness. Transformation is a natural unfolding that cannot be forced. Life is an adventure of being and becoming.

We have learned that we are energy and that we block much of that energy. As you transcend and transform your conditioning, your energy is free to release. One powerful way to release energy is in the form of creative imagery. Imaging is not magical nor is there a secret to it. We all image many times a day. Your inner images create your outer reality. A great pianist once said that he never performed without first going over every note of the concert mentally. In his mind he could hear the notes and feel his fingers on the keys.

We can develop the capacity to image with pictures, sounds, words, feelings. The more of these sensory openings we use, the more powerful and magnificent the results. Imagery is a scientific process and will work providing the key elements are there:

1. Clear the mind of its clutter.
2. Relax physically with deep breathing.
3. With singleness of purpose, make a living image with words, posture, sensations.
4. Have complete faith that what you want will come about.
5. Release the image so the energy is able to work for you.

Follow these guidelines whenever the activities direct you through guided imagery.

### Sprouting Seed

Imagine yourself as a new seed in the earth. Notice the type and texture of the soil. Experience getting the right amount of nutrients and moisture. Experience yourself eagerly sprouting through the seed's encasement. As a dynamic vessel of life, you continue to surge through the earth and grow toward the light. Come through the earth and feel the energy of the light along with the nourishment of the earth. Spontaneously assert the life form within you as you naturally unfold.

Life is an adventure of being and becoming. Experience nature's moments of chaos—wind, heat, drought, piercing rain, hail, animals, man. Persist in your urge to be and become.

Experience changes in your form as you unfold into your full potential and maturity. Experience your unique color, shape, design.

Look around and notice you are not alone. Recognize the others who have responded to an urge to be. Feel your connection. Experience the safety and joy of your unity.

Using a separate sheet of paper and a pen or pencil, describe the life form you have become. Use the present tense: for example, "I am a yellow rose" or "I am a fir tree." Then expand on what your experience means to you, what you feel, think, see, hear, touch, smell. Reflect on how this image is similar to your transformation process.

## CHAPTER TWO

# *Love and Power in Crisis*

*It is assumed that the woman must wait, motionless, until she is wooed. Nay, she often does wait motionless. This is how the spider waits for the fly. But the spider spins her web. And, if the fly, like my hero, shews a strength that promises to extricate him, how swiftly does she abandon her pretense of passiveness and openly fling coil after coil about him until he is secured forever.*
— *George Bernard Shaw*

*There is a Persian myth of the creation of the world which precedes the Biblical one. In that myth a woman creates the world, and she creates it by the act of natural creativity which is hers and cannot be duplicated by men. She gives birth to a great number of sons. The sons, greatly puzzled by this act which they cannot duplicate, become frightened. They think, "who can tell us, that if she can give life she cannot also take life[?]" And so, because of their fear of this mysterious ability of woman, and of its reversible possibility, they kill her.*
— *Frieda Fromm-Reichmann*

Men and women have the same need to belong, to be intimate, to experience fulfillment in love. Both have the need and right to own the feminine and masculine traits that lie within each. Both have a need to experience spiritual bonding, the spiritual lover. Both men and women suffer in love relationships.

We have been striving for male and female liberation for well over two decades, and though we have made some changes, they often seem to be on a social level and not a psychological or spiritual one.

The war appears to have gone underground. The amount of battering, incest, rape, violence, suicide, and homicide is on the increase. Competition, power plays, blame, and shame run rampant. I am stunned by the number of women who have been sexually abused as children and raped as adults. I'm equally horrified by the stories of men who have been sexually molested, seduced as children, and emotionally raped.

I am discouraged by the chronic manipulations and violence that occur daily between men and women, women and women, men and men. We read women are angry, men are afraid of commitment. Sexual harassment surveys report half of adolescents believe a woman walking alone at night and dressed seductively is asking to be raped. A majority of both sexes say rape is okay in marriage.[1] What this says to me is that we may have missed the point of striving for liberation. It is not men versus women, or women versus men. It is the freedom of men and women to claim all aspects of self.

If we are ever to become spiritual lovers, we must not only journey with ourselves for a while. But in that journey we need to closely examine the legacies that have created a warped view of what is feminine and what is masculine.

## THE MALE AND FEMALE IN ALL OF US

The concepts of Yin and Yang symbolize the feminine and masculine principles of life. They occur naturally and harmoniously throughout nature and are the basic polarity that is characteristic of all living systems. *Yin*, the feminine principle, is represented by all that is contractive, responsive, conservative, receptive: earth, moon, night, winter, coolness, moisture, interior. It is the intuitive synthesizing, ecologically conscious aspect of each of us. It nurtures life. *Yang*, the masculine principle, implies that which is expansive, aggressive, and demanding. Heaven, sun, day, summer, dryness, warmth, exterior, speak to it. It is competitive, rational, analytical, and more concerned with self than environment. It protects life.

The personality of each man and woman contains characteristics of the feminine and the masculine. Many Chinese philosophers believed that all men and women went through Yin and Yang phases.

Today we might put it this way: Man has a woman inside that he can come home to, one who says, "It's okay to feel, and I'll stay here with you." The woman has a male inside to come home to, that says, "I know how to go out into the world and return to take care of you." Love and power are in balance.

Many cultures viewed and programmed women to be passive and men active. Some of these cultures see the active as more valuable than the passive. It seems someone has to be up and someone has to be down.

Yin and Yang are not moral concepts. Both are good, and a dynamic balance between the two must be maintained in each man and woman. Throughout nature, the passive times are equally important as the active. We can see this by simply observing the seasons. What is harmful is imbalance, and imbalance seems to be the norm as we experience love and power in crisis.

## COMMON THEMES IN OUR STORIES

Hundreds of men and women have shared their stories. Some things are clear. Men and women alike have been abused, misinformed, abandoned, scared, and used. We have all suffered traumas as children. When important insights, experiences, and permissions were kept from us, we suffered traumas of omission. Or when significant things were done to us, things we did not ask for or deserve, we suffered traumas of commission. We carry the memories associated with these traumas of omission and commission into our adulthood and re-create that history in our love relationships today—even though that is not what some deeper, more enlightened part of us wants.

Notwithstanding the exceptions, the stories of men and women present common themes, namely that the feminine and masculine are out of balance. Outwardly, men are encouraged to be independent—frankly, antidependent at times—and women to be dependent. Psychologically, however, men are encouraged to be emotionally dependent, especially on women, and women are encouraged to be emotionally independent and not have needs met by men. An interesting scheme.

What that adds up to is a double bind for each sex. Men, often manipulated by Mother and rarely having bonded with Father, may fear being engulfed, controlled, or tricked. At the same time, they may have an underlying fear of abandonment. Failing to bond with their fathers and having been psychologically left or abandoned by their mothers, women, by contrast, may have a consummate fear of being left or abandoned, along with an underlying taboo against intimacy. A primal fear of getting sick, going crazy, or dying may be an even deeper fear for both.

These patterns run deep and have occurred for a long time. To get an eagle's eye view of the situation, we must examine the biological implications, historical roots, religious teachings, and cultural roles that affect our psychological makeup. And then, we must discover how our psychology translates into the confusion we may have about love and power.

## BIOLOGICAL PERSPECTIVES

In the relationship between men and women, there appears certain biological constraints that can contribute to the evolution of inequities we currently experience. In this process, nature is neutral. It doesn't care if the most powerful person is a man or if society enshrines female beauty. It doesn't care about our achievements or how much money we accumulate. Nature cares only about the evolutionary process. If a species does not regenerate, life stops! This requires a biological mating, a coming together, a moment of cooperation when a male and female unite.

This seeming paradox, differences between men and women, produces a miracle of life. And yet could it be that here's where fear, jealousy, anger, scarcity thinking, the basis of power plays began? Let's examine.

Relationships began as a biological function, according to anthropologist Helen E. Fisher.[2] A female experienced a period of heat and became sexually aggressive. She attracted males to her in large numbers. A mature female had only a few cycles before getting pregnant. She would refuse males until after weaning her child, at which time her sexual desire would reappear. In nature's scenario, it is clear who was in charge of procreation.

Fisher talks about how, in the evolutionary process, the female estrous cycle changed. She came back into heat sooner and was interested in sex for longer periods of time. She was then followed and protected, and became more desirable to men. She began getting rewarded for having frequent sex and, because of the special benefits of male protection, her child was more likely to grow into adulthood. Natural selection began favoring females who resumed sexual activity soon after delivering their young. Gradually, the female began losing her specific period of heat and, with that, became available for sex at all times. Life was fundamentally changed.

Males and females began exchanging favors, dividing labor, according to Fisher. Regular sexual mating began tightening the "knot" and creating an economic dependence. It soon went beyond the point of sex for procreation. The females began looking at their lovers and chose not only good lovers, but males who were good hunters, who exhibited strength and the ability to care for their young. Nature and conditioning continued an interplay. Both men and women began rewarding what they liked, what pleasured and protected them.

Personal relationships, the foundation of the family unit, began as one male and one female pairing off and sharing what meat was hunted and what vegetables were collected. Babies began bonding with the man who slept with the mother, and he in turn began to watch over the child. According to Fischer, the sex contract had been made. For the male this brought a double bind. Though the female was more available, her period of ripeness was masked, obligating him to mate more regularly to guarantee offspring.

With partnerships, sharing, and sexual bonding came displays of human emotions. Perhaps because the male wanted to protect his genetic heritage, he became jealous and possessive. Why would a man want to hunt for someone else or protect someone else's child? Because a female and her offspring might not survive without the protection of a mate, she may have experienced fear of desertion. Perhaps love games began when people experienced the fear of engulfment and abandonment.

Perhaps biology plays a big part in our present day fears. For though these fears may not be rational, they can continue to control many love relationships.

Positive emotions came along too. Altruism evolved perhaps when humans, striving to survive, recognized the importance of helpful friends or mates or because the spiritual lover was emerging. What remains for us is recognizing that both hunters and gatherers are important to our survival.

## HISTORICAL PERSPECTIVES

How did we emerge from a place where we were once peaceful hunters and gatherers and begin hoarding and fearing each other? What keeps us from sharing as emotional and spiritual equals?

### Peace and the Sharing of Power

Such questions did not always have the same urgency. We have heard legends and myths describing idyllic relationships between men and women. We know about Adam and Eve, who lived in a garden of bliss. The legend of glorious Atlantis, the fabled island in the Atlantic Ocean, spoke of a golden race who tilled the soil in peaceful ease. Human history suggests we did know moments of peace, abundance, conscious living, where people shared power and loved freely; where powerlessness, abuse, battering, and fear were rare.

---

*Chalice, blade, grail, sword*— these words are often used to speak metaphorically of our history.

- *The chalice* symbolizes the power of the universe to love—to give and to nurture life, the feminine principle.
- *The blade* is symbolic of the power of the universe to assert. It is order, it is protection, it is the masculine principle.

---

- *The Holy Grail* has been interpreted to mean attaining our highest spiritual potentialities.
- *The sword* holds mythological significance in that it speaks to the power of action needed to face our fears and darkness, as symbolized in the slaying of the dragon, which refers to the power to protect all of life.

All four are significant and important to men and women, for they symbolize the best aspects of our feminine and masculine selves.

Problems have occurred when the power of the blade has been exalted so that violence kills the life symbolized by the chalice. Think of it as, power kills love. *Take* versus *give* is a fundamental problem in this equation.

### Ancient Crete: A Partnership Society

Any society that regards the feminine principle as secondary has disregard for all forms of life, including the earth. Domination and obliteration of life then follow. Such societies exhibit a high degree of violence and low tolerance for touch and intimacy in their personal relationships.

Anthropological finds suggest that at least some of our ancestors understood on a deeply spiritual level the relationship between life and death and the interrelatedness of all forms of life. Such was the story of ancient Crete. According to Riane Eisler, from about 6000 to 2000 B.C., the people of Crete lived with reverence for life.[3] There were no wars. The supreme deity, the giver of life in many myths, was feminine. Though not perfect, this society exemplified a partnership where men and women were equal in a world that was becoming increasingly warlike.

The culture had a deep appreciation for sexual differences, seeing them as a source of pleasure. That appreciation diverted aggressiveness and promoted a harmonious sexual life. The culture exhibited a passion for sports, dance, art, creativity—all of life, both masculine and feminine. The significance of this culture is that it was the last technologically advanced society that can truly be called a *partnership society*, one in which the life-affirming, generative, creative powers of nature were highly valued.

### The Beginning of Western Civilization:
### Losing Touch with the Feminine Principle

Eisler talks about how a gradual shift was occurring in the world as the more idyllic Crete went about its business. Waves of invasions by nomadic bands from arid lands disrupted the balance of nature. Dominance, violence, destruction, and hierarchic structures, based on private property and male domination, were growing in these nomadic cultures. Metal was no longer used to make implements for protection or gathering food; instead, it was used for lethal weapons that would enslave and control people. Women were reduced to male consorts or concubines—private property. Gentler men and strong women were devalued. The balance of feminine and masculine was no longer encouraged.

The old Cretan culture and the newer male-dominated cultures were polar opposites. This fall of Crete three thousand years ago marks the beginning of Western civilization as recorded in the history books. It's from these books we teach our children about values and religion. And it's here we gain our definitions of love and power.

We've been a heavily masculine world for much of those three thousand years. One exception occurred in the twelfth century, the time of the great legends. In these legends, man was in search of the Holy Grail, his mystical, his reflective, his receptive aspect. At this time great art—spiritual consciousness—attempted emergence. The art of courtly love—a more mystical, spiritual love—emerged.[4] Relationships and romantic love were viewed as coming from the soul, the heart. We had glimpses of the spiritual lover that valued both the masculine and feminine.

### To Understand Present Relationships,
### We Must Understand What Was Lost and How We Lost It

There are rhythms in life. We are in the midst of change. It is important that we do not assume that what we know is all there is. If we do, we are in trouble. The prevailing beliefs that have run our relationships originated in domination thinking. This view sees a warrior as someone who goes to war, plunders, conquers, controls. An enlightened view, by contrast, sees a warrior as someone who seeks knowledge and can live that knowledge fearlessly. The blade cuts to affirm life, not to take it. The spiritual warrior makes love a sword.

There is no question but that the energy and roles of both sexes are indispensable to the growth and survival of all of life. Men and women are both the chalice and the blade. Men deserve the freedom to claim the feminine life-supporting aspects within themselves; women deserve to own the masculine, the cutting edge of strength, to gain protection by asserting themselves.

Our biology and history are not the only factors in this imbalance. For many people, religion has also played a role.

## THE ROLE OF RELIGION

It has been said that there are two ways to develop wisdom: (1) through nature and (2) through religious tradition. In this regard, some religious traditions have led us down the path of destruction versus the path of knowledge in our love lives. Rather than helping us develop the spiritual lover, where love and power exist in harmony, religion has too often kept it from us.[5]

There have been times when images of women have dominated religious thinking and other times when images of men have done so. In the process, birth and mother love were sometimes seen as royal powers, and sometimes as vulnerability, weakness, and dependency. The male was depicted as exhibiting a reverence for life, a willingness to establish a procreative partnership with the female, and a desire to protect and care for life. Yet at some point, man began believing he alone created and controlled life.

We seem to have moved away from a creation-centered spirituality, where both man and woman owned the divine inner spark and lived directly and simply with nature. In that direct living, each brought the spiritual lover into relationships. The kingdom of God did not refer to a territory to be owned or controlled. It referred instead to the dignity of each person, to man and woman as equal parts of the total creation.

Such religious traditions affirmed the creative force within and provided "soul food." They provided opportunities to ritualistically experience the seasons of our manhood and womanhood and to realize our spiritual potential. Their intent was to help us be spiritual lovers with ease! Ego began contaminating religion when religion became a patronizing system that supported oppression, punished creative thinking, and interpreted God as a punishing male who was often more on the side of men than women.

### How Men's and Women's Roles Came to be Defined

Much of Western civilization draws on the Bible for its metaphors that define the roles of male and female. This began in the Old Testament with the Book of Genesis, which spanned from the tenth to the fifth century B.C. Here the male is depicted as in control. Sons and their wives live in the father's household. When a woman's husband dies, his brother or another male figure assumes control over her and often marries her. Men have complete sexual freedom within and outside of the marriage, yet the wife is to be absolutely faithful. The husband can divorce but never the wife. Daughters are the property of their fathers.

The story of Lot, in Genesis, Chapter 19, shows how a father not only allowed his daughters to be violated, but he offered them to the enemy to appease them. A similar story in Judges 19:1-25 describes a threatened Levite turning over his concubine when his house was surrounded by enemies. He "laid hold on his concubine and brought her forth unto them; and they knew her, and abused her all the night until the morning." Not only does the Levite look away, he in a sense is okaying gang rape and sleeps through it.[6]

For 2,500 years God was a male figure and only men were priests. Some of the most powerful metaphors were used to divinely justify the subordination of women. Though the Old Testament tells stories of heroic women, the subliminal permission of males to misuse females remains powerful, creating confusion and victimizing both men and women when taken as universal truth.

Early Christian groups were made of small circles of people living the values of Christ. These matched the values of later Judaism: mercy, compassion, gentleness, responsibility, and helping the vulnerable, the poor, and those who were unsupported. Jesus taught the divinity of all people. He placed these values higher in importance than wealth and position. Though these values are central to Christian doctrine, strict codes and rigid thinking often resulted in suppression, domination, and fierce competition. Such discrepancies show the paradoxical presence of love and hate in our religious institutions that have guided our relationships.

Perhaps repulsed by the libertine sexual and sensual behaviors of the Roman Empire, Christianity began restraining emotions and sexuality. Aversion to sex became dogma, and woman was often identified as the problem. Saint John of Chrysostom wrote that women were to be avoided because the mere sight of them caused so much physical anguish. Saint Paul asserted that "the passions in fact are all dishonorable." Later, Saint Augustine said, "The body of a man is as superior to that of a woman as a soul is to the body." Saint Thomas Aquinas elevated the image of body, saying that women as well as men are made in God's image and likeness. Yet, he referred to women as misbegotten males via the Greek philosopher Aristotle.[7]

Even more extreme examples of domination have occurred in the name of religion: disembowelment, use of the rack, burning of witches, religious wars. How can a tradition revering virginity, asceticism, and domination help men and women create a spiritual union that applauds both sexuality and spiritual love?

Such conflict is not present only in Western religion. Buddhism, a major spiritual force in the East, was concerned about human suffering and condemned the active power plays of war, cruelty, and violence. If some interpreted this to mean denial of life, desire, and feelings, they stopped co-creating with life.

It's true that most religious people have rejected these negative influences and affirmed the values of equality and cooperation. It is imperative, however, that our spiritual lover see what negative influences still remain. For we desperately need to take what's best from our religious traditions and rituals to guide and sustain us, and leave the rest.

## Men Can Be Victims Too

Both men and women can be enslaved by negative religious ideologies designed by the contaminated ego that comes from the learned self. Not only can women be victims, men can be victims too. Men may be controlled by the illusion that they must be in control. Countless men have privately confessed to the limitations of this belief, to the impossibility of living up to it and sustaining the energy it requires. This belief can keep man from being a child with needs, a lover from the heart. For it is man who has traditionally been sent to war, to kill, to pillage, and then told to not feel the experience. With that, his spirit often dies. How can he experience his gentle, nurturing side?

## Toward Religious Spiritual Traditions

Men and women can—and are—creating something else in religion. Creation-centered theologies are helping to bring out the spiritual lover in each man and woman. According to such theology, each moment in a relationship has the possibility to be a creative one, where a spark of awareness lures us to pure intimacy, unconditional love, and unequivocal equality.

To me, sin can be defined as that which blocks the spiritual lover in ourselves and others. It is that which turns our beauty, our spiritual radiance into something that denies life. Anything that harms or injures our full humanness is sin. When man and woman alike have negative impressions of themselves, of each other, of love and power—here is sin.

In contrast, religious traditions that support the fullness of self and encourage men and women living in harmony are spiritual. Perhaps *spiritual traditions* are in need of a paradigm that

- allows for the masculine and feminine,
- allows for God as a father and a mother and a child,
- power shares as well as power plays,
- dances Sarah's circle versus climbing Jacob's ladder,[8]
- views miracle as a wonderment of creation, not the control of it,
- is critical of the status quo versus supporting it.

We need religion to look at how it has been influenced by biology, history, culture. We need to develop religious traditions that support our natural unfolding as men and women, capable of creating partnerships steeped with wisdom, love and power, where creation symbolized by the feminine and procreation symbolized by the masculine abounds.

## POWER BASES—A CULTURAL PERSPECTIVE

As a result of the influences described in the previous section, men and women may have gradually lost contact with their inherent power and looked for it outside of themselves. Rather than being our inherent life energy, our spiritual essence, power is now often assumed to be in a role we play. And each role has a base. Consider, then, what has been most easily available to men and women. Though all power bases are now available to women, I believe women continue to have three known power bases they can count on: sex, beauty, and motherhood. I believe men, by contrast, have the possibility of fourteen they can count on: finance, judicial, government, education, medicine, technology, industry, labor, communications, military, religion, professional sports, safety and law enforcement, and science.[9] With this apparent imbalance, some women may use their bases to the hilt. And some women protect these bases. The tragedy is that they disadvantage themselves and other women in the process.

### The Power Base of Parenthood

We can see the power base of parenthood in the daily life of families. Ann, a teacher, complained endlessly about her husband not spending enough time at home. She demanded shared parenting and household tasks. Ned at one point quit his job, went back to school, and shared the tasks equally. Yet, Ann responded with depression alternating with rage. "This is my territory, stay out!" she shouted. "I feel like you've crossed my boundaries. I asked you to be here, but frankly I resent it." She feared the loss of motherhood, her perceived power base.

Some psychological research shows that the number of hours men spend with their children declines in proportion to how independent and competent the mother regards herself. From this research, it's clear that mothers can provide a gatekeeping function and have difficulty allowing or inviting fathers to spend large amounts of time with children. According to the research of psychologist Frances Grossman, a father is more likely to step in when a mother is not as competent in her role.[10] When some women work outside the home, they tend to develop a supermom character, which compels them to be both mother and career person rather than sharing parent responsibilities. Perhaps continuing her traditional role helps to justify working outside the home. Or perhaps this occurs simply to monopolize parenting, one of women's traditional power bases.

Clearly, parenting is a complementary relationship. The more skillful the mothers are with children, the more skillful the fathers are as well. The father's role, according to Grossman, is affected by the mother, by her allowing him to be a parent in ways that are quite different from hers. What is clearest from the research is that neither a traditional view nor a modern feminist view of family is accurate. It's much more complex than that.

### The Power Bases of Beauty and Sex

From the power base of parenthood, we can turn to others, those of beauty and sex. A majority of women worry about their weight. Yet, the average woman is five to ten pounds within her range of normal weight. Cultural pursuit of thinness has become a raging health problem. Women continue, however, to place a basic value in how they look.

Some women continue to use sex, beauty, and motherhood to control and manipulate. Watch the advertising, turn on the TV, read books.

Beauty, sex, and motherhood are a woman's birthright, a natural part of what is feminine. A woman deserves to experience them fully right from her core, not just as a means to an end. A warped sense of these power bases has a devastating impact on the relationships with men and other women. Women who misuse these power bases betray their sisters, their daughters, their sons, and the men in their lives.

The tragedy is that many female survival tactics only reinforce the status quo. Consider how much money is made out of sex, beauty, youth, food, diets, image, clothes, home decorating, parenting. Who makes it? And notice the subliminal messages we see in advertising: seductive women and images that promise sex with success.

Women who collude with this system hurt themselves and other women. It is important to see how they perpetuate a domination model when they ask for outrageous divorce settlements, allow themselves to be controlled, refuse to learn about financial management, and make beauty, dieting, and aerobics a compulsion. Are they in fact saying, "I agree to be male property; you can buy my codependence"?

### More Words to Empower Women

As a woman and mother, I tell other women: Stop waiting for men to change. One fact of nature cannot be denied: We represent the life-bearing principle. As those capable of bearing children, we have an enormous impact on the lives of both sons and daughters. Consider yielding— know when to assert and when to let go. Accordingly, we can do much to reach our full womanhood, heal our wounds, and claim the fullness of who we are.

We have power in ourselves, not merely in sex, beauty, and motherhood. Like it or not, right or wrong, women who are parents spend more time with and often have more direct influence on their children. We can pay more attention to how we raise them.

We must stop looking outside of ourselves for fulfillment and stop inviting our sons and daughters to care for us at their expense. We must develop and share with them our internal father and mother. When we have problems we can say to them, "I'll take care of me so I can take care of you." We must do our part to invite our sons to full manhood and our daughters to full womanhood, to let them be children first and yet not stunt their growth.

## Men and Power Bases

> *The male in the past twenty years has become more thoughtful,*
> *more gentle, but he has not become more free.*
> — Robert Bly

Men also have their part in the imbalance of power that prevails. Some men have continued to monopolize the power bases given to them—or taken by them. Some men continue to inflict private, emotional violence on women: aggressive acts, intimidating behavior, teasing, demeaning remarks, unequal pay. Many women continue to feel oppressed and abused by men and report feeling angered by suggestions that they are someone's property. Outside the home as well as inside the home, power sharing is rare; the spiritual lover is missing. If you were asked who has the money and power in our world, how would you answer? Outside the home, many women struggle daily for their place. Outside the home, most women do not act out of choice despite what we believe.

The ultimate paradox here is that men are bound to their power bases, and thus are controlled by them. They must make the money needed to support women's power bases: beauty, sex, and motherhood. How many men have become workaholics? How many women in traditionally male power bases do likewise? Each sex's struggle in this vicious cycle is great. What is intended to be a win becomes a loss for both.

Let me be clear. *Power bases are not good or bad. They are intended to be means by which we can experience our meaning and creativity, to tell the world who we really are and what we do well.* Healthy love recognizes that power lies within each of us, both men and women. What creates problems is hoarding, believing the illusion that I am my role, that I am my power base.

### Both Sexes Have a Part in Abusing Power Bases

Which came first? Does a woman misuse her power bases because she's been abused, considered property? Or does a man abuse women because he's been hurt and injured, because he's not psychologically free to be straight with fear and anger? Does it really matter? Must we answer these questions before we can stop the insanity that is occurring in our relationships?

Let's face it: Both sexes have a part in abusing power. Both must change if we are ever to know healthy love again. Sexual techniques, self-help books, communication classes, couple counseling, and how-to advice of all kinds will not do it alone. Each person must help by changing from the inside out.

*The Effects on Men of Being Dominators*

Men as well as women are handicapped by their cultural conditioning. Men are supposed to have all the answers to life's puzzle by age eighteen so that they can take care of themselves and others. But how can they take of others when men don't even know themselves and what they need?

According to poet Robert Bly, a father spends an average of ten minutes a day with his son, usually giving a directive such as "clean up your room!"[11] When men began working outside the home, their sons lost a role model, the chance to have a father as a teacher and mentor. Instead, men may focus on climbing the corporate structure and competing. Men are not hiding; they are numb, and they learn this early in life. Grief is present in many men. Perhaps it's grief over a loss of their fathers; perhaps it's a loss of their connection with nature as they go into concrete office buildings. At any rate, men are taught to deny their grief. And yet in order to heal they must descend into that grief.

So there remains a hole in the male psyche. He needs older male mentors, but often cannot find them. In the process, men lose the true definition of warrior: not someone who will kill life, but someone who has a cause, a purpose, who is in touch with his soul and able to transcend himself.

Even today, Bly says, younger men can have a male mentor to "mother" them, praise, guide, and give wisdom. This mentor can teach them to reject the idea that all men are in competition and to acknowledge that men are hungry for the guidance of an older man who won't shame them. Many men are raised on shame and guilt. Man must find the king in him, the part that connects to God. This takes place in steps: The man can bond with Mother and Father, then separate from both. As such, he is free to know the best aspects of his feminine and masculine self.

It is important for men to see if and how they have been injured by the dominator model. That model has allowed and encouraged the engulfment of entire cultures and alienated both men and women from their source of personal power, their places of partnership.

Men can acknowledge what other men are doing and consider how it is impacting their love relationships. Healthy love is compromised in these cases:

- when men fail to recognize that sexism has not disappeared, it's only gone underground;
- when they protect their fears of abandonment by acting "as if" the women in their lives are equal;
- when they are not dealing with the fear, grief, and anger inside;
- when they fail to be aware that up to one-third of women are sexual abuse victims;
- when they are silent against the abuse of women, children, and minority rights; and
- when they fail to develop meaningful rituals that affirm the male's rite of passage into manhood.

## PSYCHOLOGICAL PERSPECTIVES

Perhaps by now you have gained a sense of perspective and can view the misunderstanding between men and women as far more complex than you earlier thought. We bring our biology, a millennium of history, religious influences, and a cultural heritage to our present-day power bases. Add to this the more immediate influence of our mothers and fathers, our psychological parents who have been influenced themselves by all of the above factors— usually without realizing it. They may not know and perhaps cannot know how removed they have become from their true nature.[12]

### The Male Child Raised by Parents Lost in Their Roles

Though this may seem extreme, consider the psychological dynamics when the object of a child's first love, Mother, acts as if she is inferior and Father is superior. The male child is drawn to take care of Mother and may develop a false sense of power and a disregard for the feminine power in himself by stuffing feelings and identifying with a system that doesn't ask for what it needs. His true need for nurturance and affection may often go unmet, or it is suppressed.

Often, Mother will abruptly push her son from the breast when she recognizes that he is a male child. If this is not enough, the betrayal of Father can follow. For though he is asked to join the fraternity of adult men and leave his mother, he is also encouraged to be Mom's little man, to take care of her while father is away. Though given elite status socially, emotionally he often feels abandoned by both parents.

Such a male child is in a double bind. He must abruptly leave the source of his nurturance, strokes, his first love object, but he's told by a father who is busy in the outside world to not leave. Mother makes it easy by seducing her child with her unmet emotional needs for the father not being there. Nonverbally, Mother says, *Come close, go away, come back.* Dad says, *Stay away, don't leave, go away.* The male child has a narrow path to walk: fear of getting close and then being engulfed, and fear of abandonment. But if he does it right, he may inherit the love of another woman when he grows up. The paradox is that, so raised, his psychological development does not allow for intimacy. Sexual expression often becomes the acceptable outlet for the need to feel and be close.

Many men later discover an inner rage: it's one that they often don't understand, one that cannot be expressed in direct ways to either Mother or Father. How can this boy be expected to grow up into full manhood, into a spiritual lover? Is it any wonder that so many attempts to satisfy the human hunger for warmth, intimacy, and closeness go unsatisfied?

### The Female Child Raised by Parents Lost in Their Roles

And what of the female child raised by parents lost in their roles? For her, the path to adulthood can be much different. She may learn that the object of her first love, her mother, not only acts inferior, but she is the daughter's role model. It is from her mother that she learns how to nurture and to be beautiful and sexual. If Mother prefers men to women, Daughter quickly learns the value of gaining men's attention. She is encouraged to establish a special place in Dad's life, but not more special than Mother's.

The father's attention is very significant in his daughter's development. When he affirms her, she might learn to empower men for her good feelings. If he doesn't affirm her, she is encouraged to persist in the fantasy that some day another man will. She may be groomed to look for worth and attention outside of herself, to belong to someone rather than with someone. Often, the love she experiences becomes conditional on her pleasing others—as long as she plays the game, she believes she will be rewarded. Father has been groomed to suppress his needs for nurturance and disregard the feminine in himself. Thus, he is not prepared to affirm his daughter as an emotional equal or to fully bond with her, even though some enlightened part of him wants to do so.

The result may be a woman who both needs and hates being needy. How can such a woman grow to full womanhood where love and power merge? Not having an opportunity to develop her masculine power, which allows her to go out into the world, she may fear abandonment. Never having bonded with her father, she is likely to fear intimacy or believe it's prohibited. Yet, she may continue to look outward for fathering. She, too, experiences a double bind. From Father, the message is, *Don't be close*, which results in fear of—yet longing for—intimacy; from Mother, the messages are, *Don't be separate* and *Fear abandonment*.

Here are two stories. The first story graphically illustrates how a male child can be taught by his mother and father to both fear and desire closeness. The second story shows how a female child can be raised by a father and mother to doubt herself, to fear abandonment and, at the same time, to reject closeness. These stories show the power of our heritage and psychological influences. Perhaps there is a message here for you. Even though these stories may not be ones you directly identify with, you may recognize the themes in others you love or relate to.

### Robert's Story: *The Angry Man*

> Financially I'm successful. Socially I look good—three children, a wife, and all the amenities of life. My parents

never physically abused me. They did a lot of the right things parents are supposed to do. Neither was chemically dependent.

God forbid I tell anyone about the anguish I've felt much of my life. My secret goal is to be free of my fear.

My wife wants an emotional commitment from me. Rightly so. I just can't seem to give it. I balk at intimacy. And yet, I have that awful fear of losing her. I hate how she has become my security, how I depend on her. I crave physical closeness and refuse it. I can be sexual but not loving. I fantasize about other women. I've had affairs.

It's been hell, it's been depressing. How do I know what love is? How do I get to joy again? Guilt and fear, love and hate, dominate or be dominated. I feel like a boy at times, angry and yet hoping my mother will be there for me.

I was the oldest child in my family. My mother was very unsure of herself. She used to tell me how much she loved me, how cute and smart I was. She nursed me to past age two. She had a poor relationship with her father but respected his intelligence. Men were people who women had to depend on and who treated women insignificantly. My dad was away most of my first three years. All of this left me as Mom's little lover boy. My fear—no terror— started here.

I remember somewhere around age two my mom having me in bed with her. It felt warm at first. Soon the pleasurable feelings turned to fear as she clung to me. She pulled me into her breasts for me to suck on. I felt confused. I wanted to get away. I wanted to feel her softness and enjoy the good feelings I was having. I struggled to pull away. I heard her say, "Don't you love Mommy?" I was terrified that if I left to go play, she wouldn't love me anymore. So I stayed.

This was the first time I was seduced by a woman. But I won't admit to this memory because if I do the guilt and shame will be beyond belief.

It didn't take long to discover who the real kid was—lonely Mom. As insecure as she was, she seemed overpowering to me. So I gave in, felt terrible, and promised myself in the future I'd get her. It's no surprise that I was always sexually aggressive toward women.

To add to this confusion, as I grew older Mom would say, "Men are disgusting; all they want is sex." I felt a lot of rage and wanted to hurt her. If she knew how I felt, she might leave, and I still needed so much from her. *Why won't she grow up and take care of me?* I thought. And I hated being close. Sometimes it felt like she was in my body. The way I dealt with my anger was to hold out and not give her what she wanted.

And where was Dad in this mess of growing up? He was gone most of my first three years, and after that he was like a drill sergeant, a far cry from the coddling I got from Mom. He was a big man I didn't want to mess with. He only acknowledged me when I excelled, and so I excelled. He confused me too. He resented the attention I got from Mom, and yet by his absence he forced me to displace him. A displacement I didn't want!

I wanted to scream out at him: "I won't do your jobs any more. You are a coward, I hate you! You're never here! I need you!"

My dad treated females differently than males. I noticed how he made my mother and sister wait on him, how he would flirt with waitresses and other women. If a woman was grumpy, he blamed it on her not having good sex often enough. The first time I spent alone with my dad he took me to a bar and set me up with a call girl. I felt like I was a little boy. I was so disturbed by this experience and the sexual feelings I had that I decided to separate my brain from my body. I became a robot.

I now realize what my mother did to me was awful, my dad's absence a betrayal. I was a victim of insidious emotional abuse. I am angry at my father for turning me over to my mother. I am angry that my mother preferred me to her husband. I still harbor guilt and shame and fear. I am grieving my lost childhood. I am working to forgive. I know they were victims too.

My relationship with my wife is improving. I'm less afraid of others' anger. I recognize how my fear of being engulfed and fear of abandonment result in a push-pull going back to my mother. I am being kinder to myself, more compassionate, loving, and giving. I'm looking for men who can help me figure out how to be a whole person again. And it's hard work. But let me tell you, the moments of freedom I do have are well worth it. Through my efforts, I no longer feel angry. I have come a long way.

The preceding story demonstrates how a boy-child was raised to both love and fear women. Early seduction, come close, go away, invitations to take care of Mom at his own expense, Father not being there—it's a story I have heard hundreds of times.

### *Janet's Story: The Hollow Lady*

I am four. My father is showing slides of the most recent family vacation and holiday gatherings. He flashes an image of me on the screen. I am proudly modeling my new pink chiffon Easter dress and matching bonnet. I squeal with delight, "Wow, I'm pretty!"

I was not prepared for my father's reaction. He shut off the projector and glared at me. "Don't you ever say anything like that again!"

I felt shame and believed I had done something terribly wrong, but couldn't understand why; I thought I was pretty. My mother told me so. When I asked her why Daddy had been so upset, she muttered something about him not wanting me to become conceited.

At about the same time in my life something else was happening. My father would often look at pornographic magazines. I noticed how he didn't notice me when he was involved with them. To get his attention, I would need to look and be just like the women in those pictures. I made some decisions that I carried into my adult life: Men like women to look beautiful and act helpless. Women like to look beautiful and act helpless. Looking beautiful is the most important thing in life. Since it is not okay to let anyone know that you look good, naivete is the next most important thing.

My mother helped reinforce my beliefs with comments like, "Julie should really learn to hold in her stomach." "Martha may be well developed now, but in ten years those breasts will be hanging down to her knees!" Something in the tone of my mother's voice let me know that these girls were doomed for some misery too bleak and despairing to imagine. And she always had things to say about my appearance: "You're so pretty that boys are afraid to talk to you." "If you lost five pounds, you could look just like the woman in that diet soft drink commercial."

I spent my teenage years agonizing over my appearance and poring over beauty magazines. I scrutinized the magazine models, studying their poses and facial expressions. By the time I was sixteen, I had nearly perfected the innocent seductress look. I could wear a skirt slit up the thigh and smile like a five-year-old girl: wide-eyed and naive. While my efforts encouraged plenty of male attention, the attention often seemed empty and trite.

In college, I was growing tired of fearing men and feeling like I was always performing, always posing. Yet, I was entrenched in the old beliefs that said women were help-less victims who had a right to manipulate men to get attention and what the women wanted. Men were here to be pleased (especially sexually) and revered. Women were competitors for men's limited and prized attention. Though I could never measure up to what my father wanted in a woman, I felt compelled to keep trying. By the time I reached adulthood, I knew almost nothing about honestly connecting with other people. I felt like a hollow lady desperately needing to be filled.

Something eventually gave way. I knew I had to change. I began by taking seriously my self-destructive spending and eating habits, chemical abuse, sexual addiction, and inner rage. I faced the challenge of simply being who I am in a culture that honors suffocating rules of beauty and behavior over authenticity. More of my life came from the inside of me—the essence of my true beauty. And yet often a panic overcomes me. At age thirty I fear growing old. At times I feel four again and imagine my new husband leaving me for one of those women's bodies my dad used to see in the magazines.

The preceding story is an example of how a father and mother can encourage a daughter to believe she is powerless and dependent, and to rely on sex and beauty to get what she needs.

## TASKS FOR MEN, TASKS FOR WOMEN

Much of our pain can be healed. Men can own and heal whatever wounds were created by women in their lives, wounds that resulted in their fear of engulfment. They can fully acknowledge and experience any fear of abandonment. Their rage and grief can be owned and expressed—the rage and grief for the father who did not welcome him into manhood and for the mother who kept him for herself. Then, they can find a male role model who affirms their inner life. They can, with the blessing of the women and men in their lives, develop the feminine traits of softness and receptivity, marrying both feminine and masculine aspects of themselves.

Women can own and heal any wounds inflicted upon them by the men in their lives, wounds that resulted in their fear of abandonment. They can fully acknowledge any fear of intimacy. Women can acknowledge their rage and grief over not having been affirmed by Father and the rage and grief of Mother's collusion with a system that denied equality. Each woman can find a mother to model and ritualistically welcome her into full womanhood. And, with the blessing of the women and men in her life, a woman can also develop the masculine and feminine aspects of herself.

In short, men and women alike can develop an internal father and mother and stop unrealistically looking outward for fathering and mothering in their relationships. Both can learn the real meaning of love and power.

**Seeking Balance**

The movement is changing. I am encouraged by the number of strong women who fully enjoy the wonderment of the feminine principle and continue to express personal power in an honoring way. The woman in harmony with all aspects of self is most likely to influence her daughters and sons in ways that encourage an inner balance of love and power that is so necessary to life.

I am equally encouraged by the men's consciousness movement. More men are gathering to create support groups that explore mythology and provide rituals that welcome them into manhood. Older male mentors are stepping forward to provide models that affirm what it means to be a healthy male. More men are willing to express their masculine aspect and not at the expense of their feminine side as they express their spiritual lovers.

**It's First Necessary to Marry Yourself**

The personal stories in this chapter illustrate an important fact. Before I get married I need to marry myself, to develop the best aspects of the masculine and feminine. Before people can take part in healthy love relationships, either homosexual or heterosexual, they each must have the courage to take the blade and cut the invisible yet strong umbilical cords that keep them from the fullness of self.

They must face the dragon—the limiting beliefs and habits that have run their lives for generations. With the conviction of warriorship, they must love and nurture themselves, even though they might not like what they have become. They must develop into spiritual lovers.

This will be a struggle at first because so many have yet to develop their internal mother and father. Their spiritual lover's light is barely visible. Their faith may be shaky. Each needs a mother inside who says, *I know how to take care of you; your needs and feelings count.* Each need a father inside who says, *It's okay to trust what you know. I know how to protect you. I won't leave.* Both will say, *I'll teach you what you need to know to feel safe in the world, to become who you are intended to be.* Listening to those words, each of us can transcend the negative influences of biology, history, religion, culture, and psychological enmeshment. The greatest challenge we face today is in this healing. To begin the healing, we are called to look at our life of illusion, our script that we may have taken as our truth. This will be the theme of the next chapter.

## ACTIVITIES

### 1. Discovering the Masculine and Feminine Energies

We have learned that each of us contain the potential of our polar opposite: The female embodies potentially male energy, the male the feminine. The rational houses the intuitive, the adult nurtures the child within. In claiming our paired opposites, we create wholeness. Here is a list of characteristics. Check those that most pertain to you. Mark an "x" by those you would like to express more often. Remember, to develop inner father/mother we need both. Work toward balance and wholeness. Know that there will be times for both the male and female. *It is the female in us who opens the door to our inner wisdom. It is the male in us who acts on this knowledge and brings it to the world.*

| **Masculine**<br>(Sword, Hunter, Ego) | **Feminine**<br>(Grail, Gatherer, Spirit) |
|---|---|
| Active | Passive |
| Closed | Open |
| Competitive | Yielding |
| Analytical | Intuitive |
| Forceful | Soft Spoken |
| Self-Reliant | Open to Nurturance |
| Assertive | Empathic |
| Strong | Tender |
| Risk Taker | Cautious |
| Identifies with Sun | Identifies with Moon |
| Leader | Follower |
| Protective | Nurtures |
| Concerned with Death | Concerned with Life |
| Expansive | Contractive |
| Progressive | Conservative |
| Self over Environment | Ecologically Conscious |
| Identifies with Heavenly | Identifies with Earthly |
| Athletic/Physical | Sensual |
| Directive | Responsive |
| Decision Maker | Loyal |
| Determined | Hesitant |
| Cold | Warm |
| Ambitious | Humble |
| Strong Willed | Easily Lets Go |
| Pragmatic | Aesthetic |
| Structured | Flexible |
| Rational Adult | Feeling Childlike |

By owning and confidently expressing our feminine-masculine energy, we are free to develop the ideal inner father and mother that we've needed all along. Rather than our addictive lover looking for the perfect woman or the right man to feel complete, we attract the man or woman who reflects our wise inner parent. Indeed, we will not entrust our self to anyone less. The paradox is that as a woman owns the wise male in her, it is safer for her to visibly show her feminine nature. And man discovers that connecting with his feminine power, he is more secure in and free to express his maleness.

## 2. *Developing the Inner Father and Mother*

Review the list of characteristics on page 62. From this create the ideal image of a father and mother. If need be, look to people you know and respect who give evidence of the best aspects of the feminine and masculine. Then do the following exercise.

- Relax, deep breathe. Go within your mind and bring forth an image of the ideal mother, whose strength you feel in her nurturing and wisdom. Take the time to explore her. Notice how you feel in her presence. Should any negative feelings or concerns enter your mind, dialogue with her until you feel safe.
- Bring into your mind the image of the ideal father. Again, notice how you feel. Should any concerns or questions be present, ask the wise father for what you need to feel safe. Dialogue until you are satisfied.
- Notice how the inner father and mother feel to you in each other's presence. Tell them what you learned about mothers, fathers, love, power, and relationships in the past—how this parenting may have failed you or left you feeling incomplete.
  - Talk about the hurts and injuries, the wounds of love. Tell them the good parenting you received and want to keep.
  - Image entrusting your inner child to them. As a man, do you feel safe giving your child to the woman? As a woman, do you feel safe releasing your child to the man? Because of the hurts and fears, you may not readily turn over your inner child. That is okay! Do this exercise as many times as you need to have your inner child trust your inner parents.
- Complete the image by symbolically bringing all of your parts together—the injured child, the emerging adult, and the wise and loving parents.

## CHAPTER THREE

# Healing: From Script To Autonomy

*To be born again is to take the
Responsibility for being the father
and mother of my own values.*

—*Sam Keen*

We are creatures of habit. We have learned how a multitude of influences in history have contributed to these habits, both good and bad. We cannot go back and relive the past. What we can do is look to see how the past is still here in our psychological makeup and is keeping us from expressing love with power.

It has been said in numerable ways that we are the creators of our own reality, that our outer experience is but a reflection of our inner reality. We have in our life what we intend to have, and what we don't have we don't want. Some will deny this truth to avoid guilt or personal responsibility. Frankly, I find this to be good news. Knowing that I am in charge of me gives me a vantage point. I no longer need to look outside of myself for a sense of wholeness. I no longer need to have others change for me to be content. I no longer need to control.

Most relationships are in trouble because the need-clouded self insists it is incomplete and searches for a "someone" or a "something" to feel happy. This self forms an emotional attachment to a love object, to a habit, to a thought, or to a favorite bad feeling.

## UNDERSTANDING OUR INNER CHILD, WHO DETERMINES OUR IMPORTANT DECISIONS

How do we come to feel incomplete? To answer, we need to understand our inner child. The seed potential of our wholeness resides within the child part of our personality. This inner child represents our life energy, our urge to grow. It identifies needs, wants, feelings. It requires a responsive environment that affirms its rights and teaches it how to live in cooperation. This child never leaves us and can be stopped only by death itself. Often, however, it is depressed, suppressed, or made unimportant.

This part of us records life traumas and the responses to those traumas. It thinks in black and white and can easily personalize life events: "This always happens to me." "I'll never get what I need." "I disappoint people." The child was once willing to trust itself, others, and life and closed down only after it got burned. It is not rational and it surveys life intuitively. It attracts people and events that fit its inner beliefs or, when such attractions are lacking, it will create them.

*Most importantly, it is that inner child who determines our most important decisions*—or who can pull the plug even when a more enlightened part of us wants something else. It is essential to understanding scripts that we take seriously every life event the child in us has felt good or bad about. It is through these experiences we decide about love, power, men, women, life. As adults, we can and must illuminate and heal the injuries the child has suffered. We must examine closely the beliefs it sustains and change those that keep us from what we say we want. Many of our beliefs may have come to us via generations of men and women, and we may resist change.

The stories presented thus far help us see how the inner child acquires a learned self and denies a deeper identity. Those stories also show the psychological power we had as children to make decisions. Though the options available were limited, even then we did have choice. Those choices become adaptations, a way of life that at best provides us with banality, lives of ordinary people. From time to time we make contact with this void, the boring, empty quality of life.

**Why a Certain Imbalance Is Necessary**

The paradox is this: Our birthright is to get everything we need; yet if we got everything we needed, we might not grow. Unmet need is a motivator. For example, Adam needed Eve, the feminine principle, to feel discontent. Yet we should not view Eve as an evil temptress. Such imbalance is necessary to call attention to a need. We need this to challenge us and continue our spiritual growth. That, indeed, is part of the excitement. The truly spiritual person is one who fully experiences the darkness of temptation. It's not script versus autonomy. It's script, then autonomy—to release that which once protected us and now blocks us from a deeper knowing.

## THE NATURE OF LIFE SCRIPTS

We, too, can experience our inner darkness. In order to claim who we are, we must first discover who we have become. As emphasized earlier, we must realize that we bring three selves into any situation or relationship: the addictive self, the autonomous self, and the spiritual self. In turn, these manifest the addictive, healthy, and spiritual lovers inside us. We can further understand one of these selves—the addictive self—by looking at life scripts.

It has been suggested that the majority of our time is spent operating blindly out of a life plan. To quote psychiatrist Eric Berne:

> Each person decides in early childhood how he will live and how he will die, and that plan which he carries in his head wherever he goes is called a Script. His trivial behavior may be decided by reason but his important decisions are already made: what kind of person he will marry, how many children he will have, what kind of bed he will die in and who will be there when he does. It may not be what he wants, but it is what he wants to be.[1]

"Scripts are artificial systems which limit spontaneous and creative human aspirations," continues Berne.[2] "Transactional Analysts did not start out with the idea that human life plans are constructed like myths and fairy tales. They simply observed that childhood decisions, rather than grown up planning, seemed to determine the individual's ultimate destiny."[3]

Sigmund Freud referred to the repetition compulsion. Carl Jung refers to archetypes and the persona. Other well-known psychological theorists refer to this as well. Alfred Adler said, "If I know the goal of a person, I know in a general way what will happen." R. D. Laing used the word *injunction* for strong parental programming. The idea that lives and dreams are patterned by myths, legends, and fairy tales was recognized by Otto Rank and is eloquently presented in Joseph Campbell's *The Hero with a Thousand Faces*. Each of these thinkers, in his own way, was contributing to the foundation of life scripts. Indeed, some spiritual thinkers say we enter life with a specific temperament that has the potential to be both our vice and our virtue. The mystic says, "You have abandoned yourself to your false personality. You have a veil of illusion."[4]

This life plan, or script, is predictable. It provides a sense of comfort and grounding. It is a composite of our early life experiences reinforced with later experiences. It becomes the frame of reference through which we view the world. The plan is as unique to us as our fingerprints, and yet we too easily assume others view the world from this perspective too.

Think of the life script as the protective outer shell of a seed. Initially the seed greatly benefits from this protection. In the same way, we design our scripts in childhood to keep us safe, to protect our vulnerability. We adapt to the world, not with the intent of dishonesty, but because we know of no other way to care for ourselves. If Johnny is rewarded by Mother for lying to the bill collectors, he may learn to be dishonest. When Sally is given attention by being coy with Dad, she may become a seductress. Children will do whatever is needed to feel safe, to get strokes, to have predictability.

How often have you promised yourself that you would not say or do something only to turn around and say or do it? How many times have you felt driven by an inner compulsion? How many times have you said you want love and continue to find rejection?

These are the more obvious signals that we are not the captain of our own ship. We can recognize such behavior patterns even though we often don't understand the motivating force behind them. In short, we can come to terms with our life script.

## The Power of a Life Script

Cindy came to me in a deep depression and had strong suicidal ideas. The problem, she said, was her fiancé's inability to make a commitment. Each time they discussed marriage he would break off the relationship, only to return a few weeks later asking for reconciliation. Originally, Cindy wanted advice on how to get her fiancé into therapy, so he could look at this pattern.

Consistent with my belief in the "100 percent intent ratio," I began exploring Cindy's frame of reference to see why she had chosen the partner she did. In describing him, she said, "He's a really nice man, but he's rarely there when I need him most." She had been married one time before, and in describing her former husband she used almost identical words: "You know, he was a really nice guy, but he was rarely there when I needed him most."

Once is an accident, twice is coincidence, and three times is a pattern. And so, doing regression work, we went back to a scene where Cindy, under age six, was observing her depressed, melancholy mother. I asked her why she believed her mother was crying. "Because," she replied, "my dad is a traveling salesman and isn't home very much, and my mother misses him."

"And what are you concluding about men?" I asked her.

And she said, "Men are really nice, but they're never there when you need them most."

There was that internal belief, one that supported her continuous choice of men who are emotionally unavailable. Cindy learned that this belief, which had an element of truth in her childhood, clouded her vision of men. Her autonomous self was open to love and intimacy, and her spiritual lover was ready for bonding. Yet, her learned self would either choose partners to fit her belief or sabotage loving relationships.

It was important for Cindy to accept fully who she is. Even in the pain she was experiencing, it was important for her to recognize that her ego was a loyal friend, that its intent was to protect her from harm. That part of herself had to be gently guided to a different way of viewing life and men.

## WHAT DOES YOUR SCRIPT LOOK LIKE?

A life script is the basis of both the addictive lover and the learned self. Unless it is changed by a major life event or gut-wrenching redecision, we are likely still operating from such a plan.

It is said we spend most of our time, perhaps 95 percent, "in script." Whenever we do, we are prone to addictive love, meaning that others are in charge of us, psychologically speaking. When we are in script, we are discounting some aspect of ourselves and others. Whenever in script, we have an emotional attachment to our experience. And, it has been said, that even after learning about our script, we are invited into script a majority of the time. When in script, we are on automatic pilot, because what drives us is, for the most part, unconscious.

The more you know about your life script, the more options you will have in your relationships. This knowledge is a useful way to maintain healthy boundaries as you begin to recognize your vulnerabilities. Such knowing allows you to develop an observer's self that steps back, recognizes familiar behavior, and guides you to better choices.

Recognizing our script in the here and now seems essential to moving out of our denial and into our autonomous self.

### Script "Positions"

Let's look at a process model of script. The word *process* here means always in motion. This model can help us recognize where we are from moment to moment.

There are four aspects of the life script, often called script "positions." We spend some time in all four and can quickly move from one position to another. Each of us, however, seems to have one preferred position where we spend much of our time. The model is based on the mini-script theory of Taibi Kahler, Ph.D., and Hedges Capers. I've linked their theory with that of Robert L. and Mary McClure Goulding's "Script Injunctions" and overlaid it with my own ideas.[5] What follows is an explanation of each position. You'll no doubt recognize a few familiar places.

| | |
|---|---|
| • Driver Position | • Vengeful Position |
| • Payoff Position | • Stopper Position |

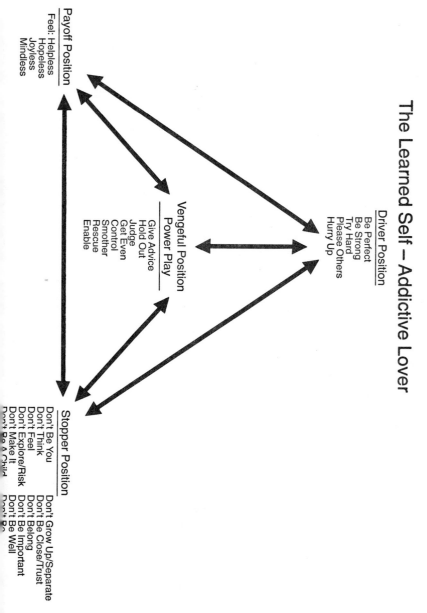

# The Learned Self – Addictive Lover

**Driver Position**
Be Perfect
Be Strong
Try Hard
Please Others
Hurry Up

**Payoff Position**
Feel: Helpless
Hopeless
Joyless
Mindless

**Vengeful Position**
Power Play
Give Advice
Hold Out
Judge
Get Even
Control
Smother
Rescue
Enable

**Stopper Position**
Don't Be You
Don't Think
Don't Feel
Don't Explore/Risk
Don't Make It
Don't Be A Child
Don't Grow Up/Separate
Don't Be Close/Trust
Don't Belong
Don't Be Important
Don't Be Well
Don't Be

71

*Driver Position*

Position One is called the Driver Position. Here, we feel compelled to act in specific ways. Verbal messages from the past and present haunt us: "You should do better." "You're not doing it right." "You're not good enough." "You can't let them know you're weak." "You'll never get it done." Such messages from authority figures drive us to *be perfect*, to *try hard*, to *please others*, to *be strong*, and to *hurry up*. These people lead us to believe that esteem, importance, love, and power are conditional on specific behaviors. And, as we adapt, we are adequately rewarded with smiles, hugs, praise, money, and good grades. How can we resist?

Many people spend a great deal of their time in this position. The reason for this is quite simple: When living from this position, we have a positive feeling about ourselves, others, and life as a whole. The tragedy is, this good feeling is present only if we meet certain conditions. The line we walk is narrow.

Anxiety prevails. There is an inner tension associated with the *I must, I have to* feelings. Two things are related to that tension: (1) I know what I'm being asked to do is impossible and a set up for failure; and (2) I'm using most of my energy attempting to read others' reactions since some part of me believes they're psychologically in charge of me. The paradox is that I will be less effective because I'm misdirecting my energy by reading others' minds to determine how I'm doing.

According to Kahler, each person has a favorite driver he or she brings from childhood. We often recognize drivers in relationships.

- *Be perfect.* Jim, a compulsive perfectionist, in his uptight, precise manner, continually drives himself and others to do better.
- *Be strong.* Bill, who is tough and macho, can't let people know he's weak; in a hard, cold manner he says, "No comment."
- *Try hard.* Julie, in her try-hard mode, carries tension in her stomach and shoulders, sits forward, looks perplexed, and says, "It's really hard, but I'll really try."
- *Please others.* Dolly, a chronic people pleaser, says in a high, whiny voice and with raised eyebrows, "I don't want to do this for you" and then turns around and says, "Can I help you?"

- *Hurry up.* Andy often feels harried and beats himself up by saying, "I'll never get it done"; yet his next words are, "Let's get going."

Drivers are a persona, a mask that cannot be sustained for long. As we drive ourselves with self-effacing comments and internalize someone else's disapproval, or what we think might be disapproval, we eventually go to Position Two, the Stopper.

*Stopper Position*

Here, we are reminded of the prohibitions of childhood—nonverbal messages that tell us that some aspect of who we are, what we feel, need, think, or do is not okay or unimportant. We commonly experience one or more of twelve such powerful injunctions, as identified by Bob Goulding, M.D., and Mary McClure Goulding, M.S.W.[6]

> *Don't be you—be what I want you to be.* What you do reflects on me. I wish you had been a girl (a boy). Girls are seductive. Boys are busy. Be good. Be perfect for me.
>
> *Don't think.* I'll do the thinking for you. Don't disagree and don't trust your own thinking. You're dumb, you're stupid.
>
> *Don't feel.* Repress your feelings. I'll show you what feelings are acceptable here. Boys don't show tender, sentimental, sad, or anxious feelings. Girls don't feel anger or excitement or show their sexuality. But they can be sad, hysterical, depressed, and nurturing.
>
> *Don't explore/risk.* Don't take chances. Play it safe. Don't explore or you'll get hurt. Here—let me put you in a harness. These are the only ways and places you can explore. I'll protect you; the world's a scary place. Don't be excited or creative.
>
> *Don't make it.* There's only one top position here and it belongs to me. I'll make sure you fail by giving you tasks and not the skills to do them. I'll laugh at your mistakes. I'll give you compliments and take them away.

*Don't be a child.* Hurry up and grow up; I need a helper. I'm too depressed to take care of you. My needs come first. You'll have to wait until others are taken care of. I don't know what I'd do without you.

*Don't grow up/separate.* Don't leave me; I need to be needed. Here, let me take care of you. Look at what a wonderful nurturer I am.

*Don't be close/trust.* I'm not comfortable sharing myself with you. I changed my mind: Go away, I'm too busy. I'll hit you again if you're not careful. You're too big to sit on my lap.

*Don't belong.* You're different. Don't tell anybody what goes on around here. Get your needs met elsewhere. You must belong to someone else; you sure don't look like me. You're so special!

*Don't be important.* I'm busy, don't bother me. Compliments will only go to your head. Kids should be seen and not heard. I don't have time for you.

*Don't be well.* You're bad. You're a problem. Something is wrong with you. I'll always take care of you when you're sick.

*Don't be.* I wish you had never been born. Go play in the freeway (ha-ha). I wish I'd never gotten pregnant. I'll give you a nickel to drop her in the river (ha-ha).

These are only some of the limiting or indirect messages called *injunctions* the child in us can hear. Not only does the intuitive thinker in us get the message, but we begin drawing conclusions on the basis of these messages, making decisions that could guide the course of our lives: "There is something really wrong with me." "It's not safe to reach out." "I'll show you when I grow up." "I'm bad." Injunctions are powerful and not easily given up. In our adult life we replay them, and as we do we block our abilities and birthright.

### Todd's Story: *Come Close, Go Away*

Todd, a bright, attractive, and helpful man, complained that no matter how pleasant he was to women, he would invariably turn them off. As a child, he had learned to become Mom's little man, her helpful servant, yet she had little time for him. "Here, have a cookie and stop bugging me" was a frequent statement of Mom's. This not only communicated to Todd "you're not important, so go away," it also set up a belief system that said, *If I can't get what I need by being good, I can get Mom's (women's) attention by bugging them.* That later translated into behaviors that assured disapproval. Ultimately, Todd's familiar bad feeling of rejection could be reexperienced.

Todd could see the drama, the repetitious quality in all this. For Todd to change, he had to recognize and experience the anger he felt at his mother for the message "come close, go away" and the rage he felt at his dad for Todd having to be Mom's little man, for not being there for him. From that place, he could change his belief about himself, and the self-destructive behaviors stopped. Relationships with women became affirming.

Each of us experienced one or more of these twelve messages when under six years of age. Our options were limited, we empowered authorities, we had to survive. We could not run away. Or, if like me, you ran as far as the end of the block and the world looked very scary.

The decisions we made at this time directed us to predictable behaviors and ultimately to a bad feeling that we could identify as familiar: rejection, shame, guilt, self-righteous anger, depression, loneliness, anxiety, to name but a few. If, for example, we were shamed as a small child when expressing negative emotions, we might now opt for excitement or a false sense of happiness.

If what you feel is not accepted, a substitute feeling, called a *racket feeling* by Berne, will be played out. We manipulate the environment to be sure to have these feelings. Sometimes we even "collect" those feelings, storing them until we have enough to justify some folly: an affair, suicide attempt, depression, a good drunk, or a flare of anger.[7]

Some people spend most of their lives in the Stopper Position, where they've learned to control the environment by being a martyr, a victim—sick, insecure, needy, dumb, unimportant, depressed. In droves, others are drawn to rescue and persecute them. Life remains predictable.

Some people despise this position and barely set foot on this ground lest they feel one-down. They may choose to go back to Position One (the Driver) where they drive themselves even harder, or else they go on to Position Three, the Vengeful Position.

### Vengeful Position

This is where the illusion of power, control, and one-upmanship prevails. Self-righteous anger and competitive behaviors are used to maintain the illusion. Here people confront others to hurt, get back at, get even, control, dominate, and get their own way.

I don't think I have to convince you that many people like this position. Once here, they have a hard time leaving. Why should they change? Up on the pedestal, they can look down and invite others into an array of competitive power plays. Advice giving, holding out, getting even, emotional smothering, and enabling come from here. So do judging, projecting, and other power plays. It is rare that people in the Vengeful Position seek help. In their denial, they maintain they don't need it. And besides, they secretly know of some darkness and fear that creep into the best people. Not real warriors, they cling to their false sense of power. This position is tenuous because what goes up must eventually come down.

The Vengeful Position protects us, however, from feeling even a deeper sense of the pain that we have experienced in Position Four, the Payoff.

### Payoff Position

Here, we find feelings of hopelessness, helplessness, joylessness, and mindlessness. This is the place of darkness where a person doesn't care about self, others, or life. Nothing matters; only darkness is present.

We go to this position originally as children when, unable to care for ourselves, we reached out to the world to tend to our needs, to respond. The responsible people, the authorities, could not or would not respond. So we felt pain for the first time—darkness. We didn't like being here and so, watching the world carefully, we designed our scripts with the hope that we would never have to come back to Position Four. The intent of our scripts was to get us back into the light.

The paradox is, all of the other positions inevitably lead to Position Four—darkness. Some people get here daily, some weekly. For most of us, however, it takes years. And, though we may think we're in the light, the light shines dimly or at somebody else's expense. And at times someone else controls the switch.

I know of no one without a personal life script. How can we fail to be affected by our environment? The question is not "do you have script?" but "how limiting is your script?" Each time we made an adaptation or a limiting conclusion, we agreed to give up some aspect of our realness, our autonomous self, our spirit. Little by little we forgot who we were, and we began thinking that the learned self was real. To shield us from the pain of this loss of self, we built elaborate defense systems. In doing so, we not only convinced others the illusion was real—we even convinced ourselves. In addition, we maintain a loyalty: We agreed to take on what our parents could not see or were unwilling to deal with in their lives of illusion.

The people I talk to often tell me powerful stories about the effects of their scripts. Following is one of them. It demonstrates how script has a beginning, a middle, and a predictable ending.

***Dan's Story:*** *"To get where I want to be, I need to let go."*

> I am a workaholic. I am struggling to develop spiritual meaning in my life. My wife is asking for a separation. My fantasy is to spark the spiritual void I feel and wake up and feel passionate toward life and my wife again. I am very successful in my own business, yet I constantly worry about failure or having to end up working for someone else.

I'm learning how I am a product of my history. I had a mother raised by a father who promised her that she would always be well taken care of by a man. My father started his own business and it failed. My mother beat him up emotionally for that failure. He became depressed and lived in shame. Memories of this haunt me.

When my father's business failed, I knew I was to take his place. Mother referred to me as her beloved son, perfect in every way. By age four, I was so removed from myself that I had a constant smile, even at times when my heart was breaking. I became a performer, and there was no shortage of praise. My mother used to sing, "Hush little baby, don't you cry." I got the message, and I learned how to hide my feelings. I needed more time with my dad, to have him hold me, read stories, hear his voice, and when that didn't happen, I would just curl up, alone with a smile. I saw Dad getting more depressed. I decided to stay detached, say funny things, and not make a ruckus!

I began feeling confused about what it meant to grow up and be a boy. I felt pulled between making Mom feel good by bringing pride back to the family and being angry at how she treated my dad. I concluded love was stress and tension. Closeness didn't exist.

I can't show my needs or feelings. I feel real sad as I recall my experience as a four-year-old, recognizing how scared, confused, and abandoned I really was. I had no idea then how these events would shape the course of my life. What I had then seemed pretty normal.

My father was rarely around. At age eleven, I captained and coached my grade school team because there were no fathers to do it. I had to grow up quickly. How lonely I felt.

My experiences with women were not good ones either. In seventh and eighth grades I joined a group of guys. We always picked the cheerleaders, the most popular girls. I felt safe in groups but never alone with girls. In junior high

I was seduced. I was so frightened I freaked out and left the party, but was too embarrassed to tell my friends. In college, having had too much to drink, I molested my date. I was so frightened I stopped dating. Next I was raped by an older woman. No good! I decided at this point that sex is dirty, mechanical, and there's no spirituality involved.

Looking back at my life, I long for a mother who has a sense of identity, self-assurance. I'd probably be more honest, respectful of women, and willing to share my emotional self. Everything would be different. I wish my father had taken better care of himself, communicated with my mother about what was going on behind his back. I weep at the distance I kept from my father whose spirit died in his shame. Had I bonded with my father I'd respect myself as a man. I wouldn't fear the failure in my business and be so driven that I now spend ninety to one hundred hours at work each week.

If I stay on the same path, I'll end up living alone and feeling extremely lonely. My health will deteriorate. Unhappy, depressed, I will withdraw more and more. I will end up indifferent to living.

To get where I want to be, I need to let go of the fear of failure and heal the wounds subtly inflicted upon me. I must forgive my parents, but not before I claim the little boy who still sits in the corner alone and grieve his losses.

## THE AUTONOMOUS SELF

Our challenge is to spend more time in a life of autonomy, our original destiny. That reality is our birthright. In actuality, the autonomous self should not have to be identified and reinforced. However, since we have been asleep for so long and the grooves of our early influences run so deep, we initially lack trust in ourselves. We often do not know which self is doing the talking. And since most of our transactions are invitations back into script, we slip from time to time, even under the best of circumstances.

When living from the autonomous self, the sense of our worth and that of others and the world at large is not based on conditions. I am accountable to myself and others. I maintain a position of emotional equality. Here, from the autonomous self, I experience a renewed passion for living and respond to primal urges: I am spontaneous. My intuition is heightened as I open to the world. Creativity works through me and I live in the present moment. My real self recognizes that the past and present are all really one. We go back to the learned self only long enough to reclaim parts of ourselves arrested in early development.

The autonomous self contains the door to spiritual awakening. Initially, however, it may be more concerned with the ego's difficulties than with a spiritual quest. This is temporary, however. It is important to spend the time that's needed with our learned self, as our autonomous self separates from the past. Here our foothold is a bit uncertain, and we need time to synthesize.

We must integrate such changes into our mind, our nerves, into the very body we live in. After all, we do live in a human body, and some say it takes six months to incorporate a change so that each cell is at one with the change. In addition, we often find present relationships changing, some outdated friendships ending, and new friendships consistent with our autonomous self beginning. We are working toward a well-integrated personality that will allow for heightened states of spiritual consciousness. Often, this starts with an inner struggle between script and autonomy. That which is a struggle, however, later becomes a dance. The dance occurs when we allow ourselves to be in script to gather more information for further change. Here, we develop an observer self who keenly watches and nonjudgmentally calls us to attention.

In autonomy, we develop the internal man and woman, the internal father and mother we've been looking for. Art describes this vividly.

***Art's Story:*** *"I could choose to care for my parents as I could choose to care for myself."*

I began to reflect on all I was learning about developing my own inner father and mother, how important that was, and how much I enjoyed it. Then in my mind a picture began to form. There appeared an old woman—dressed in a long, flowing white robe with long grey hair, blue eyes, and a beautiful, dark face filled with lines. This woman had warmth and depth. This woman was my Nurturing Parent, a spiritual mentor. And as she sat gracefully upon a large stone, holding a staff in her left hand, I noticed that she sheltered and held under her right arm two small children. The children were frightened. They huddled together, shivering and trying not to get caught, but they knew I had seen them. They were my mother and father.

The scene was serene. The old woman told me that my parents had never received the nurturing they needed as children. Now that she was giving them this nurturing, they were content.

At first I thought, *How nice that I am nurturing my parents.* But then I began to feel that this was not good at all. My inner child screeched, "What's she doing spending all this time and effort on our parents when she should be concentrating on me?"

She replied to me, "You are the boss. It is completely up to you. If you want me to let them go, I shall. But first, you must know that they are quiet now because they are getting what they need."

I told her that I still wanted her to let them go, so she did. As soon as she released them, they began to scream.

I asked my Nurturing Parent to hold my parents again and to take care of them. She did and they began to quiet down.

I now possessed the knowledge that I could choose to care for my parents as I could choose to care for myself and give myself the things that I needed. My internal parents became quiet and content. So did I.

This story illustrates how autonomy invites us to release blame so we are free to forgive and embrace our parents or others who have hurt us.

**Playing with Faces and Masks to Develop Our Wholeness**

For the autonomous self, myths provide the images and stories necessary to develop our wholeness. We value and explore all parts of the self. We claim our anger, fear, primal urges, sexual passion, and naivete. The wild man and untamed woman inside us come forth. We try on varying personalities. Archetypes burst forth. We are having fun with the ego. We play with many faces and masks and try them out for size. In our excitement, we can become mere brutes as we take the lid off of pent-up instincts. We can even trample others.

This is not always fun. As uncertainty comes, a doubt, a resistance appears, perhaps for one last test. "Are you sure you want to go ahead with this journey?" "How do you know it will be any better?" "We haven't had it so bad, have we?" "Our life was predictable before; what can you count on now?" "Will anyone be there for us after the transition?"

Sometimes we feel as though we are being crucified, arms outstretched pulled in opposite directions. Resistance is only doing its job. *Whatever we are asking the learned self to give up is what it designed for us in childhood to keep us safe and give meaning to our life.* Thank it; talk to and educate it; be patient. Soon it will join you in autonomy. Aloneness replaces loneliness, and periods of solitude are equated with freedom. This is a time of falling in love with yourself.

I recall a client who enthusiastically came into a therapy group singing, "I'm in love, I'm in love, I'm in love."

"Who's the lucky person?" responded several group members.

The answer was: "Me. I am in love, truly in love, with me for the very first time in my life!"

For someone who had had no self-love or self-respect and whose life plan pointed to sexual abuse, bulimia, alcoholism, theft, and suicide, this was indeed a celebration. Autonomy had been achieved after months of therapy.

**The Four Positions of the Autonomous Self**

In the autonomous self, there are again four positions as defined by Kahler and Capers.[8] These correspond to the four script positions in the learned self (see page 71). Knowing about these positions can be useful in understanding our love relationships as we recognize the places that feel right and honoring. And since they correspond to the four positions of the learned self, we can choose them at times when others invite us back into script. In other words, they provide us with healthier options for relating to others. The four positions of the autonomous self are the Allower Position, the Goer Position, the Affirming Position, and the Wower Position. (See chart below.)

# The Autonomous – Healthy Lover

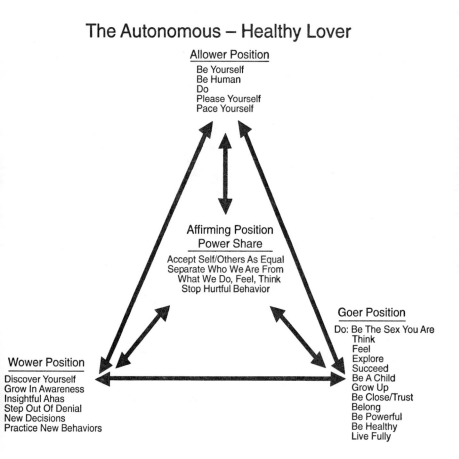

**Allower Position**
Be Yourself
Be Human
Do
Please Yourself
Pace Yourself

**Affirming Position**
**Power Share**
Accept Self/Others As Equal
Separate Who We Are From
What We Do, Feel, Think
Stop Hurtful Behavior

**Goer Position**
Do: Be The Sex You Are
Think
Feel
Explore
Succeed
Be A Child
Grow Up
Be Close/Trust
Belong
Be Powerful
Be Healthy
Live Fully

**Wower Position**
Discover Yourself
Grow In Awareness
Insightful Ahas
Step Out Of Denial
New Decisions
Practice New Behaviors

*Allower Position*

Position One, called the *Allower*, gives affirming messages to free us from compulsive conditioned "okay-ness" that we experienced in the Driver Position. Here, we move from a need to *be perfect* to the right to *be yourself*. This message tells us it's okay to be who we are, to make mistakes and to trust we will grow from them. Relieved, our body relaxes as it takes in and acts on this message. No more scrutinizing of our performance is needed.

The complementary allower for *be strong* is *be human*, which affirms that it's now okay to claim our true human nature, our feelings, and our needs. The facade—the rigid body—relaxes. Rather than *try hard*, we hear the inner voice give us permission to *do* or not do. Again we sit back, relax. Pressure eases. We do what we can do—nothing more, nothing less.

With that we take a deep breath. Instead of pleasing others, we are free to *please ourselves* and others from a position of choice, not fear. We are free to say no. The stomach relaxes. And, instead of the hurry-up *driver*, we learn that it's okay and important to *pace ourselves* for our well-being. We now can stop and smell the roses, watch the sunset, meditate with life. We are in a comfortable rhythm, and though we may dance fast at times, it's from choice. Our body flows, and we feel sensuality in the movement.

*Goer Position*

Position Two, *the Goer*, in contrast to the Stopper Position mentioned earlier, encourages us to get on with living life fully. That life comes from being who we are in the now. The internal mother and father speak to us in gentle, potent voices—unlike the limiting messages of script injunctions as defined by Bob and Mary Goulding. These voices say:

> *Be all that you are and are intended to be.* Go for it. Like the blade of grass coming through the hard dirt in the Spring, reach for the sun, know your true nature, confidently walk your path. I'm glad you're a girl child or a boy child.

*Think your own thoughts and trust your own thinking to guide you.* You can disagree, and you can ask all the questions you need.

*Feel what you feel, not what others want you to feel.* I will teach you how to fully and safely express what you feel. I'll help you trust to feel and think and act at the same time. It's okay to feel all that you feel: your sensuality, your deep primal nature, your fear, your anger, your tenderness, your grief, your joy, your passion for living.

*Explore, risk!* I will teach you how to do it safely. You can experiment and discover what you enjoy doing. You no longer have to do something to be someone. You are someone.

*Succeed as you define success.* I trust you will know what is right for you and enthusiastically experience it. And, you are free to experience far more success than I dreamed possible.

*Be a child.* Play. Have needs. Laugh, cry, joke, run, slide, jump! Feel your exuberance for living. Gently touch the plants, the rocks, the earth. Experience life with the wonderment of a child. Get nurturing and protection as you need it.

*Grow up and be responsible to yourself and to your commitments.* You can go out on your own and still know you are welcome home any time. You can live your life your way. In all areas, you are free to grow and change and it's important you do so.

*Be close /trust.* Entrust yourself into the hands of those who will treat you with value, honor, and respect. Love, first yourself, and then others as equals. Though you are free to trust, know that not everyone is worthy of your trust. At those times, trust your distrust and move carefully. Be a person others will feel safe with.

*You belong.* You have a place in the world. Decide how you belong and where you want to belong and with whom to belong. Life is a process of eliminations. Make your choices wisely and spend time where you feel safe and cared for. Feel your connection with all of the earth and its creatures.

*Be important and powerful.* Extend that power—take your uniqueness and share it with all of life. There is no one else quite like you. You make a difference. Share your power.

*Be healthy in mind, body, and spirit.* Love your body, take care to rest, eat well, exercise, take in nurturance. Feed your mind and spirit.

*Live fully.* I'm so glad you're here, alive at this time. You deserve to be here and live your life fully. I love you!

These permissions are not only heard—they are deeply felt as we make our shift in outlook.[9]

*Affirming Position*

Position Three, the *Affirming*, is called that because here, unlike in the Vengeful Position's need to be one-up, we *accept ourselves and others unconditionally as equals*. We *power share* versus *power play*. We are called to separate who another person *is* from what that person *does, thinks,* or *feels*. We will not always like others' actions. But here we continue to acknowledge and affirm the person's right to be and his or her essential goodness. Our unconditional love remains. We confront hurtful behaviors, not to hurt or injure others, but to *stop hurtful, abusive behaviors*.

This position represents partnership. Emotional and spiritual equality are fully experienced in spite of differences. Many people find this to be the most challenging position of all, for here we are called to let go and share power daily. We are asked to love ourselves, even though we are not where we want to be and have done things we regret doing.

*Wower Position*

Position Four is called the *Wower*, referring to major "aha experiences" that shift us from script to autonomy. We have insights that help us recognize our repeated patterns, our mechanical nature. With these insights we make decisions that alter the course we have taken. We continue our *self-discovery.* We read books, do therapy, join groups that support behavior changes, and practice those new behaviors. *We have stepped out of denial.*

It's likely that, during infancy, Position Four of the learned self, the Script Payoff, was the front door of the learned self. So the Wower Position, too, is the door we open to get out of our scripts. *Awareness precedes most changes.* Some traumatic life event or major insight shifts us long enough to see ourselves more objectively. As we grab on to those glimpses, we are moved to continue the search for the Holy Grail—the authentic self.

**Life of Autonomy**

Once we have made this shift, life is never the same. A life of autonomy feels right and honoring. It calls us forward to the best aspects of our humanness. We may spend considerable time in the search for identity, focused on knowing ourselves, experiencing self-actualization, developing an inner parent, and being more concerned with self than others. But this is both temporary and necessary to ourselves and our relationships.

We have opened ourselves to God, to a spiritual consciousness. Before long there is still another shift. We take fewer trips into the past to find ourselves. We are living more in the now and are more sure of our footing. Whether we are responding from our autonomous or learned self becomes irrelevant as we know we will learn from any experience we have.

We notice a change in our focus gradually moving from "I versus You" to "We." We take what we learn and walk more fully into our relationships, choices, and life decisions. We are, indeed, aware. We are amazed when we realize *we are more like we were and more different than we ever dreamed possible.* And we know what those words mean.

We ask simple and deep questions as we did in childhood:

- "If I'm so little and the stars are so bright, big, and far away, why do I feel so important?"
- "Why do I feel like the stars are my friends?"

We begin seeing plants, bugs, snakes, birds, clouds, people, land, lakes in a new way.

We begin feeling a double bind. We are at once more connected to and more alienated from life. We take more care about what we say to whom. Living in the light, we don't like all that we see and are called to live with it. The authenticity of our spirit has spoken.

## BEYOND AUTONOMY

Popular psychology of the seventies began the desperate search for self-identity. Too often, this was interpreted to mean "I" and "You" comes before the "We." Autonomy, we hopefully discovered, is not anarchy, antidependence, or doing what we want when we want to do it. Autonomy is not an excuse to fight or take our place with power plays. Nor is it a justification for self-gratifications, greed, collecting more possessions and addictions.

Autonomy comes to mean the freedom to be who I am as I am, to know what my truth is, to know what feelings in a relationship belong to me versus what I believe others want me to feel. It requires taking responsibility for my actions and the ensuing consequences of those actions. It requires living my life in ways least harmful to myself, others, and all of life. It is ethical. Autonomy becomes the discovery of my essential nature that was separated from my learned self. It is the ownership of the bruised and neglected inner child that feared love and intimacy and developed a misguided sense of power. It means developing the inner woman/man, the inner father/mother that can care for the child within me and guide it into trusting itself, others, and life again. Autonomy becomes an opening to a deeper knowing and understanding of my spiritual core.

Though autonomy, a healthy sense of identity, is important in the broader spectrum, it is not a stopping place. It is not *the* answer or *the* end. In our goal-oriented thinking, we probably believed that once we achieved autonomy our ordinary problems would fall aside. Our relationships would be easier, and there would be less pain. What we learn instead is that *easy isn't always honoring, and honoring isn't always easy.* And once we are conscious, there is no going back to the blame, shame, control, or addictions of the learned self without taking personal responsibility for these behaviors.

This step in humility, this acceptance of our life of illusion, presents a paradox. As we own the powerlessness of our learned self, we are free to fully experience the creative energy that helps us see ourselves anew: "I am less of who I thought I was and yet more than I dreamed possible." We continue in search of who we are born to be and discover what we are here to do in this life. We begin following our bliss. We begin unveiling our spiritual lover.

As people discover their realness, they develop well-integrated personalities. They speak more frequently of God, destiny, world concerns, moral values, meaning. They more frequently experience warm, close, supportive relationships that express partnership. They exude a confidence that draws others to them.

Focused solely on autonomy, however, a person remains in the material world. Had each of us got everything we needed in just the way we needed it, we would be autonomous as we left our family of origin. And yet is this enough? What, I ask myself, is beyond getting real? Is it an end in itself? Is autonomy all there is? In the seventies, many thought so. Our addictions make it look so, but is there more?

We don't have to search long for the answers. We turn to the answers in the next chapter.

## ACTIVITY

Discovering all that is within you would take more than a lifetime. Yet by reviewing your history and your development, you can learn more about your personal road map and its destination. You can examine the inner child that has been traumatized or neglected, to get a better understanding of present behaviors. Furthermore, you can create new images of the future as the real self wants it to be, and solicit the support of a spiritual lover as the wise and loving guide within.

And you can look at your favorite fairy tales, recognizing how you have been living them out on a literal level.

This can be a respectful assessment and a therapeutic journey that helps you realize how much has been endured, suffered, and made acceptable via your script.

Seeing the utility of the script and power of self-determination, you may begin a grieving process. As you say good-bye to that which has kept you safe, you may grieve the loss of childhood and the sense of wonder. You may grieve at the realization that you are a woman or a man without a father or mother.

The questions to consider are: Have we completed our child development? Have we grown up? Have we gotten all the permissions in our development to live our life fully? Are we secure in ourselves? Do we really know where we're going and why? Do we view the world, make decisions from our inner self or our outer, defined self? Are we on our own paths? Have we shed the destructive shoulds and other destructive values and attitudes—the dos and do nots—and taken on our own set of rules that are in harmony with our spiritual development?

I believe, if you are honest, you know aspects of your script and want out. You also understand the pain of knowing is short-lived because there is something greater ahead.

### Seeing the Script Process

The plans that we live by are the necessary adaptations we made when something went wrong in our development. We are incredibly flexible creatures. The child in us learned quickly to psych out the world and determine how to get what was needed. That clever psychological adaptation became a way of life and is now a part of our neurological makeup. We run on automatic pilot.

Here are more specific things you can do to discover how active your life of illusion is. Each can be an exercise in itself. Take one at a time, One Day at a Time.

- Look back to your favorite fairy tale and consider how it is like your life.

- Listen for inner words, messages that defeat love and power.
- Observe behavior patterns that produce negative outcomes.
- Look at your current relationships. How do they resemble your childhood?
- Experience the nonverbal messages people communicate and how you react.
    - Look to see what part of your history those messages are re-creating.
- Look at what is not happening in your life that you say you want.
    - Look to see what messages and decisions within you keep you from what it is you say you want.
- Look for unfinished business—things that did not get resolved in a healthy way. Finish!
- Examine your life for traumas and unusual events, along with what you concluded because of them.
- Talk with people who knew you as a child and who are willing to give you honest insight.
- Make a list of the "dos" (driver) behaviors and "don'ts" (script injunctions) you received as a child. Note how they are affecting your life and relationships now.

As you do the above, let the knowledge come to you as you are ready. Some things you may not be ready to hear or know yet.

As your script begins talking to you, decide what you want to keep and what is important to change. What you change is up to you. Consciousness does not mean you have to change everything about you; it means taking ownership of who you've become and a commitment to growing out of denial.

## CHAPTER FOUR

# Transformation: From Autonomy to Spirituality

*The divinization process which leads to transforming union, the ultimate stage of the mystic way, depends upon a healthy and harmonious individuation.*

— *William MacNamara*

What's beyond autonomy? Transcendent wisdom that we all have access to—God! The ancients knew it. So did the philosophers. And, though many dare not admit to it, so did the early psychologists. Why did it take us so long to come back to the beginning of what was already there to begin with? How did we get so far away from this knowledge?

Psychology is intended to deal directly with mental and emotional illness and dysfunctional behaviors. Yes, I can accept that. Spirituality was to be experienced in holy places—churches. Yes, I can accept that. But then I began witnessing something significant. As people began breaking free of restrictions in the learned self, they began to naturally experience and express more of their spiritual authenticity. Though they had problems, they transcended those problems and transformed themselves. They had self-love. They had personal power. They captured glimpses of the spiritual lover.

## THE WEIGHT OF OUTDATED WORLDVIEWS

Traditional religious teachers have sometimes been critical of psychology. Psychology has been described as anything from an agent of the devil to an overconcern with ego and neglect of the spiritual nature of man.

The latter we can understand. Western psychology, determined to be a science, became openly critical of that which was spiritual. Psychology took its interest in the psyche, originally meaning the soul, and began focusing on the outer covering, the persona, the mask of personality. Today, psychology has come more to mean the study of personality or mental illness than to mean study of our human nature. We have become preoccupied with the mask that is mistakenly identified as the true self. We take personality tests and psychology classes and read books to find our personality type and to learn why we do what we do.

Such a narrow focus gets us even more identified with the learned self. Why? Because we are operating with a view of the world rooted in Newtonian physics. That view basically pits humanity against nature rather than promoting harmony. It attempts to describe the spiritual from the material. From this viewpoint, human beings ultimately become complex machines, a series of stimulus response mechanisms.

How did this view come about? To answer this question, we need to understand some intellectual history.[1] A dramatic shift in world views occurred between A.D. 1500 to 1700. Before this time the world was seen as organic. There was a relationship between the spiritual and material. Medieval science used reason *and* faith to understand the meaning and significance of life.

The age of Scientific Revolution changed all that. We began viewing the world as a machine to be controlled with numbers, laws, measurements, and quantifications. With English philosopher Francis Bacon, the goal of science became to dominate, to make a slave of nature. According to Bacon, nature, viewed as female, had to be "hounded in her wanderings," "bound into service," and "put into constraint." The aim of science was to "torture nature's secrets from her."

French mathematician and philosopher René Descartes is generally considered the founder of modern philosophy. Though he claimed the existence of God, to him the universe was an elaborate, lifeless machine. His view of the physical nature of the world view could exclude that which is spiritual. Such thinking justifies destructive acts against the earth. After all, the earth is viewed as man's servant.

Sir Isaac Newton, the English mathematician and physicist, went beyond Bacon and Descartes. He thought a God created material particles, the forces between them, and the fundamental laws of motion. God set the whole universe in motion, and it has run ever since like a grand clockwork. After that point, God was not needed. The Newtonian approach to the universe became the main force of the age of enlightenment.

From there followed John Locke's "Tabula Rasa Theory": The mind at birth is a completely blank tablet. On that blank slate, knowledge is imprinted once it is acquired via the senses.

The thinking of Descartes and Newton still pervades our lives, from economics to love relationships. We see it in statements that suggest domination, control, and a preoccupation with technique. "I can control my addictions." "I need others to change to be happy." "I am the extension of my role." "What I do is who I am." These statements suggest accepting the material, concrete world as the sole reality and remove us from the inner experience of our spiritual lover.

Exploitation and manipulation theories also affect psychological thinking today. This means that psychologies that focus only on behaviors or the unconscious mind fail to see experiences of higher consciousness. They are stuck in an outdated worldview.

## A NEW WORLD VIEW IS EMERGING

*The mechanistic world view cannot make us healthy because it misses the point of who we are; conscious beings passing through an evolutionary process, creative and fluctuating in nature, and able to transcend to new levels . . . never victims of our past . . . in charge of our destiny. If we continue to focus on the objects in our life as truth we will miss the point entirely.*
— *Jacqueline Small*

A new worldview has emerged. Physicist Fritjof Capra attributes our current crisis to the failure to acknowledge the shift now occurring.[2] This shift is based on the new physics. Though this view is not shared by all physicists, a common worldview is taking shape. Quantum physics no longer sees the universe as a machine but rather as a dynamic whole whose parts are interrelated and can be understood only as patterns of a much larger process.

Simply put, the new view says life is a dance and we are the dancers. The new view affirms East and West, the feminine and masculine, the material and spiritual. It supports partnership, power sharing. And it encourages a new psychology, that of transformation.

Psychology as transformation proposes that all life events, including our addictions and painful love relationships, are our teachers. It encourages us to transcend our learned limitations. It assumes we can, with the help of all psychological forces, begin to experience more of our spiritual nature. It works to create a well-integrated personality that identifies with higher spiritual forces and a personal experience of God. *This new view says that it is our level of consciousness that has the greatest impact on our relationships.* It views us as a channel of higher spiritual wisdom and says that we have the capacity to tap into that wisdom.

From this new perspective we can see the brain as a hologram. A *hologram* is a three-dimensional image made by reflecting light from an object. This image is composed of many smaller images that are exact copies of the whole. In the same way, our brains encompass the whole scale of our reality. The English poet William Blake wrote of this:

> *To see a World in a grain of sand,*
> *And a Heaven in a wild flower,*
> *Hold Infinity in the palm of your hand,*
> *And Eternity in an hour.*[3]

To know ourselves in the deepest sense is to know the universe. And if the universe includes a transcendent reality, then so do we.

### WHEN RELIGION DIFFERS FROM SPIRITUALITY

*Western civilization has preferred love of death to love of life to the very extent that its religious traditions have preferred redemption to creation, sin to ecstasy, and individual introspection*

> *to cosmic awareness and appreciation. Religion has failed people*
> *in the West as often as it has been silent about pleasure, about the*
> *cosmic creation, about the ongoing power of the flowing energy*
> *of the creator, about original blessing.*
>
> — *Matthew Fox*

Traditional psychology has tended to take a dim view of religion. I can understand why. For some people religion became but a hiding place, a place to avoid being real, a desperate attempt to escape aloneness and the human condition, to stay unconscious. For some, religion can be a way to stay in denial. It's been a place to judge others, to keep other people in their place, to be self-righteous and one-up on others.

When religion only serves and perpetuates doctrinal systems, it is only religion, not spirituality. It is an extension of our conditioning. When religion refers to a system of beliefs and traditions, binding our spiritual nature with a slavish dependence on God, we have created yet another addiction.

## WHEN RELIGION IS SPIRITUALITY

*Religion* is a linking of the spiritual nature of man with the transcendent, the sacred. It allows for the experience of heaven on earth. In the words of American poet Henry Wadsworth Longfellow, true religion is "the great world of light, that lies behind all human destinies"; in the words of Shakespeare, it is the "treasure of everlasting joy." This religion allows for the experience of ecstasy, bliss, and a sense of harmony with all life. It views prayer not as a mere act of beseeching but in the words of Mother Teresa, "God speaking in the silence of the heart." Here both nature and spirit commune.

Religion is that which guides us to the realization that my personality is not who I am; rather it is something I have. It guides us to the knowledge that we can transcend the suffering that has resulted in our addictions, habits, roles, and pretensions. It confronts the abuse we experience in relationships. It guides us to our true nature that contains the seed of spiritual consciousness, the opening to God.

### The Meaning of Repentance

The path of spiritual development in a certain sense is a path of repentance. Adin Steinsaltz eloquently presents the paradox of repentance. In *The Thirteen Petalled Rose*, he writes that in the Jewish concept of repentance, a person must liberate her- or himself from all alien influences and gradually overcome the "forms engraved by time and place before he can reach his own image."[4] In other words, a person must break free of the chains, the limitations, and the restrictions imposed by environment and education. In this view, remoteness from God is not physical distance but spiritual distance.

In repentance, each of us must turn away from the pursuit of what we crave in our desires in order to reach for the divine. When we do, there will likely be a time we feel cut off from the past. This is the moment of turning. Here a major metamorphosis occurs. The sharper the turn, the more prominent the release of the past, the transformation of self, and the eagerness of moving forward will be. Repentance is not only a psychological phenomena but also a process that can effect real change in the world. Repentance can be viewed as a thrust to break through the ordinary limits of self and return to the spiritual self.

### Many Roads to the One Destination

Many religions have seen that we need mythology and rituals to help grow into our manhood and womanhood and into our sacredness. Yet, spiritual life may not always be found in a religion. Nor is religion always reflective of the life of spirit.

There are many roads to the one destination of God. Spiritual people do not judge others' paths unless it puts a roadblock in theirs. Even then, the spiritual person judges without being judgmental and walks around, perhaps even through, the roadblock. Our religious path is up to us. Perhaps if we were all fully in tune with our spiritual nature, we would not need a path. We'd discover we are the path.

## REFLECTIONS ON MY OWN SPIRITUAL PATH

I was raised a Catholic and still identify with many of its rituals and deep spiritual truths. I've examined world religions and studied principles of metaphysics, been intrigued and transformed by the Fourth Way teachings of Gurdjieff and Ouspensky, and been fascinated and harmonized with Eastern philosophies. I seek counsel from a Catholic priest, a retired minister, and a wise woman.

What may appear eclectic in my spiritual path, even scattered, is not. As seekers of truth, we must fearlessly and openly explore and experience the knowledge of differences to discover the similarities. For inevitably, like a sieve, the mind lets through that which is truth. I soon learned that there is a universal knowledge that transcends the specific structures called religion, philosophy, and ways of knowing. True spirituality is all of the above and more. All paths speak to that which is divine within us and gives food for the spirit.

As an explorer and questioner, I had to discover for myself what religion and spirituality was and was not. I can tell you what I believe religion does not do.

- Religion does not tell me I am bad and how to be good. It affirms my goodness, my naivete, and my transgressions as fully human and as lessons to be learned.
- Religion does not say, *This is the only way, the truth, and the life.* It says, *The way, the truth, and the life are all here within you.*
- Religion does not say, *This is the only way to know God.* It says, *You are a child of God and have whatever you need within you to live a life of spirit.* It doesn't serve systems. It calls me to a deeper level of living within the system.
- Religion does not control with fear. It guides me gently to the wonderment, the amazement of life and God. It does not damn and imprison me in my pain, suffering, and unwise choices. It trusts I need those experiences to learn.
- Religion does not count and measure deeds and require specific giving. It invites the yearning of my soul to love and serve others. It doesn't discipline because it thinks I need punishment. It disciplines to stop the ego long enough to know the joys of spirit.
- Religion does not say, *Choose this religion or that one.* It says, *Your daily life is your sacred school.*
- Religion does not say, *You have to achieve to get to heaven.* It says, *You experience heaven in the moments of rapture, wonderment, ecstasy, and service.*

## LIFE IS TRANSFORMATION

The book *A Course in Miracles* describes our search for heaven as well as anything.

> *There is no need for help to enter heaven for you have never left. But there is need for help beyond yourself as you are circumscribed by false beliefs of your identity, which God alone established in reality.*

Michael started with the intent to reform, to fight his history. What he did, instead, was transform his way of life. He changed from the inside out.

*Michael's Story:* "*As I release my script and what I think I should do, my spirit moves more freely through me.*"

My journey started when my father was born. It started there because he was a central figure in my early beliefs. He learned a script steeped in conservative Catholic tradition. He was taught that man is basically flawed. He learned we are suffering servants and any undeserved suffering is redemptive. *Suffer he did.*

My father met and married my mother, whose sense of self was absorbed in the man she married. They became one in a real sick way. I entered their life. My life became an adventure that I had no idea would carry me to the places I have been.

I was a first child and was baptized by a priest, the family "holy man." From a very early age, I was anointed by Dad as a priest for the family. I was sure priesthood was for me. Suffering, adventure, a missionary! That had it all. After high school graduation I joined an order of missionaries. The next year was the first significant change in my spirituality.

In that year, I spent most of the time closeted from the rest of the world. I really tried to be a priest. Be it as it may, I didn't want them and they didn't want me. I was terrified. Leaving meant *letting God down*, not fulfilling my obligation. Most of all, I failed my father.

My flawed self took over and formed a vision of God as super-cop in the sky, looking for my sin and demanding perfection. He was scary. What a tightrope walk!

As I look back, I see such a needless, desperate picture. A young man so full of desire, passion, promise and yet so torn by his own divisiveness. He moved only to please others in hope of assuring God that all was okay.

My way out of the mess was to marry someone who was "good enough" for my father and God. And so I married the daughter of one of my father's friends.

I was sure this would put me in good stead with everyone. I was miserable. But then I thought, *Being miserable is suffering, and I was put on earth to suffer. If there is no sin, I must create one.*

These thoughts were outside my consciousness. I started "acting out" and didn't know why. I believe it had to do with a script that mandated mistakes, suffering, redemption, atonement, and then perfection. With perfection never there, the cycle would start again. Protecting my core of shame became a full-time job.

I was well on my way to dysfunctional living—trying to be perfect, yet irresponsible and blaming God. I was in a spiritual and emotional desert. And then my father died. With his death, I looked at my mortality and knew that this life has an end.

I kept going to church but only as a habit. I became cynical, cold, and detached from family, friends, myself.

On my fortieth birthday I woke feeling broken. I decided things must change! This call was from inside of me. It was a spiritual stirring. To know my spirit, I had to strike out on my own path, free myself of outdated "shoulds" and "ought tos" prescribed at birth. I had to embrace my shame, which then paradoxically dissolved. I gave back my father his script, his life of illusion.

This left just me and God. As my self-esteem increased, God seemed to soften and become more human, like the George Burns character in the movie *Oh God*.

I have a mission statement for my life that reads:

I am committed—
To know who I am.
Be free to be that person.
Develop the courage to be that person.
To act on my truth, my values as I know them based on *my* "wise inner guide."

My "wise inner guide" once came to me in a dream in the form of two six-foot white angels, who spoke as one. I believe it was divine intervention, for that dream moved me in some very important directions.

The form I know as God has changed as I changed. When I felt bad, God was angry. When I owned my goodness, I experienced God's love and power. As I release my script and what I think I should do, my spirit moves more freely through me.

My view of God today is the same as Zorba in the movie, *Zorba, The Greek*. When asked "What is God?" Zorba answered, "God? God is just like me only . . . much larger and much, much crazier." Who am I? I am Michael, a one-of-a-kind, therefore divinely perfect, a radiant child of God.

**A Life of Authenticity: To Transform, Not Reform**

Abraham Maslow said that there are two kinds of self-actualizers: nontranscenders and transcenders. The first type of person remains primarily in the ordered world. These people "talk the talk." They change from the outside in. In relationship counseling, they want the specific how tos to get desired results. They have few experiences of transcendence. They attempt to actively reform the world.

Transcenders, by contrast, become transformers. Transformers change from the inside out. Illuminations from their inner experience help them shift their views of self, love relationships, and the world. They "walk the walk." Having undergone a personal transformation, they know firsthand that we are all one. They respond to addictions and power plays in relationships as opportunities to grow. With that knowledge, they aid the world as they gently and confidently walk the earth. They transform, not reform. They are committed to a life of authenticity—to being spiritual lovers. This has been called the transpersonal level of being. It includes all of our inner reality—the learned, autonomous, and spiritual selves.

## POSITIONS IN THE SPIRITUAL SELF

Here is my conceptual model designed to help our human self reflect upon what's beyond autonomy. Just as there were four positions in our learned and autonomous models, likewise there can be four in our life of spirit. In them, we are challenged to express our spiritual lover:

- Transcending
- Being and Becoming
- Loving
- Awakening

## The Spiritual Self – Spiritual Lover

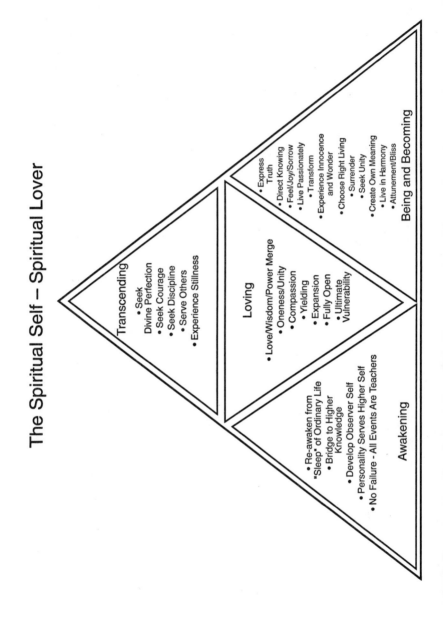

**Transcending**
- Seek Divine Perfection
- Seek Courage
- Seek Discipline
- Serve Others
- Experience Stillness

**Loving**
- Love/Wisdom/Power Merge
- Oneness/Unity
- Compassion
- Yielding
- Expansion
- Fully Open
- Ultimate Vulnerability

**Being and Becoming**
- Express Truth
- Direct Knowing
- Feel/Joy/Sorrow
- Live Passionately
- Transform
- Experience Innocence and Wonder
- Choose Right Living
- Surrender
- Seek Unity
- Create Own Meaning
- Live in Harmony
- Attunement/Bliss

**Awakening**
- Re-awaken from "Sleep" of Ordinary Life
- Bridge to Higher Knowledge
- Develop Observer Self
- Personality Serves Higher Self
- No Failure - All Events Are Teachers

## Transcending

In *Transcending*, we are functioning out of a sense of knowing what is right. Here we master divine truth and operate from intrinsic values that are much different than the rules that govern the majority. Our values are self-generated, self-directed, yet universal. We discover here that living a life of spirit requires much of us. Having claimed our autonomy and divorced ourselves from the learned self's need to be perfect, we freely *seek divine perfection.* Rather than being a compulsion, this is an inner response to the urge to be all that we can be, to use our power to manifest the seed of our potential. I want to be the oak tree, the flower. If I'm an artist, I want to be the best artist I am seeded to be. If I am a mother, I want to be the best mother I am seeded to be.

Once we're comfortable with being human and having emotional needs, we experience the call to *seek courage.* Unlike the learned self's drive to be strong, in this courage we feel a power deep within that allows us to face pain and fear. We continue our development as we do hard tasks. We walk through our problems, not around them.

Having given ourselves permission to do or not do, we discover the value of *discipline.* Unlike the learned self's push to work hard, discipline is viewed as a structure that all sacred schools provide to encourage the development of that which is spiritual and not ego dominant. Though we may have many ways to discipline our body, we also need to train the emotions and mind so they are working for us, not against us. For example, one person may do even routine housework with spiritual consciousness, as a training to develop clarity and awareness. Another may deliberately go to the end of a long line to develop patience. Or someone may memorize four lines of a sacred verse and use them to calm the mind in the presence of suffering. *This type of discipline never blocks or attacks the appetites of our human self.* That would be control, which ultimately leads to repression. Instead, this training teaches us to redirect and constructively channel our energy.

We move from wanting to please ourselves to wanting to *serve others.* Unlike the learned self's drive to give or please others from a position of fear, the spiritual self calls us to give to others from our soul. Learning how to serve others can be a powerful way to transcend our own human suffering.

Even in the midst of our pain, we can begin experiencing the joy of serving. Giving becomes a living prayer. It is not codependent. It is not "saving the world" or martyrdom. It is genuine caring and serving of humanity because we know we are all mirrors to one another. Here, the giving and receiving are one and the same. Experiencing the plight of the world calls us to give, each in our unique way. We give something each day without calling attention to it. We do a healing deed and feel a power in it. All of our relationships then benefit.

Having stopped the frenzied and hurried life of the learned self, we move from pacing ourselves to times of *stillness*. In this experience, we begin to understand the true meaning of Let Go and Let God. This slogan calls us to do our part fully, whatever that is, and then stop and trust the universe to do the rest. Stillness is a living meditation where our human and spiritual aspects meet.

Sometimes we are active in our stillness. In the state of mind Zen Buddhists call *satori*, the spiritual warrior emerges. This happens when the mind is free of thought, when the emotions are open and free. Though the body is active, it remains relaxed. Stillness is when I really feel centered. I need these times to let in the bits of insight necessary to my growth. There is balance, flow. This is all part of transcending.

## Being and Becoming

> *I don't know whether my consciousness is proper consciousness or not; I don't know whether what I know of my being is my proper being or not; but I do know where my rapture is. So let me hang on to rapture, and that will bring me both my consciousness and my being.*
>
> — *Joseph Campbell*

One of the greatest challenges we have in life is to be "in the world but not of the world." Our learned self adapts to and is defined by the world. We agree to stop being who we were born to be. As we shatter the parental prohibitions of our past and claim our birthrights, our spiritual nature unfolds.

In *being and becoming*, we activate our spiritual nature. Having access to transcendent wisdom within ourselves, we now make every effort to live it. Conscious living is the theme. The power to create our meaning is realized. We walk into the world unafraid. When someone confronts us, we have the freedom to yield. We do not criticize the world. We do our part to live in it as an enlightened human being. Having transcendent wisdom does not mean leaving life but living it fully, passionately, with a new level of consciousness. Simply put, the soul has entered reality. Ego (I) and Spirit (Thou) create a partnership, a new me. I take up the sword and chalice in their deepest meaning.

Knowing and liking who we are, we are free to *express our truth.* We "walk our walk." Now free to think our own thoughts, we experience *direct perception,* an inner knowing. Free to feel, we express joy, sorrow, ecstasy, and other *higher emotions.* Free to risk and explore, we use intuitive wisdom to *live life passionately.* Knowing we are successful, we *transform.* Claiming our inner child, we return to a sense of *awe, innocence,* and *wonderment.*

With permission to be a responsible grown-up, we choose right living versus living right. *Right living* comes from that inner knowing rather than an outer set of rules. Knowing intimacy with others and trusting ourselves, we can now *surrender* to the process of life. We not only belong—we directly feel *unity consciousness,* a holographic (three-dimensional) experience. Grounded in our sense of personal power, that inner life energy, we are free to express our life force and *create our own meaning.* Love with power directs us and keeps us on course. Health translates into *harmony* of mind, body, and spirit. Living life to the fullest, no longer overwhelmed with relationship questions, ordinary living, pain, fear, or darkness, we experience a feeling one might call bliss, or rapture. Life is in full *attunement.*

## Loving

*In personality we are many; in essence we are one.*
— *Jacqueline Small*

In *Loving,* we move beyond the autonomous self who has learned to affirm itself and others. Power sharing has replaced competitive power plays of the learned self. We have separated who a person is from what the person thinks and feels and does. Now, we espouse emotional and spiritual bonding with others. We have found the heart and opened it widely. We love as deeply as a human can love, experiencing closeness and intimacy far beyond enmeshment.

From this opening, the expansion of total love begins, and our spiritual lover emerges. In primary relationships, loving from our spiritual lover can be so profound that it catapults us into heightened states of consciousness. In a sexual union, that opening can be so complete that orgasm can be experienced in stillness, with no action required.

The opening to our primal urges shifts the energy into the heart and out of the body. In marriage, each person sacrifices the ego to a union greater than any ego can experience or imagine. We may experience a profound sense of *oneness;* we may experience a love, a passion for *unity* with all of life that goes beyond our primary relationships. In the giving we experience receiving.

One recognizes *the power of love as it merges with will and wisdom.* Love is spirit expressing itself. It is spontaneous. Love is the impulse of life that comes from the heart. Love is a state of being that knows no limits. It requires no specific love object, though there may be one. Love sublimates life into a spiritual plane of experiences. Power is no longer feared as it has expressed itself in its greatest form—love and kindness. Here is the spiritual lover.

### Awakening

The move from autonomy to the life of spirit is an inner awakening. It's that point in time where somehow we develop full awareness of who we are in the here and now. This is really a *reawakening*, since we were born with this awareness. Again, we are at one with the universe as we *become* the totality of who we are. Like the blade of grass, the oak tree, the rose, we claim our true nature. We know the real meaning of authenticity, love, and power. Personality is now called to serve our spiritual self.

This higher state of consciousness becomes the *bridge to higher knowledge.* Our experience is being met head on, fully embraced. We are in tune. The words *see, hear, think,* and *feel anew* come to life. This is direct experience, no more partial understanding. No more attainment, it's attunement! It's joy versus achievement. We experience our core, the essence of life that connects us with all that is wondrous. We make our decisions from this core, and the decisions feel right and honoring.

Here, we *develop an observer self* that not only cares with detachment but is a spiritual mentor, a God-self. We take walks with our mentor; we go inside and listen for the messages:

- *Stop pretending your life is ordinary.*
- *You don't have to do anything but stop agonizing.*
- *Decide what you will do and not do.*
- *Examine what fears are stopping you.*
- *All teachers are students and all students are teachers.*
- *Pay more attention to your partner.*
- *You are doubting.*

The wise guide is a connection with universal, divine intelligence. We begin channeling this information in our life in many ways. As our ego steps out of the way, the wisdom flows through us. Often, we'll get bursts of words that just seem to come through us. At those times, we know we've just tapped into a source of knowledge much greater than we are. In that regard, we are all channels. We don't need to have someone channel for us. Tapping into the great divine is our birthright and heritage.

## THE SEED OF SPIRITUALITY WITHIN AN OUTER SHELL

Life is a journey from no boundaries to boundaries, to no boundaries again. The paradox of returning to our spiritual self is that we return to a place from which we started, the place where our problems began. When we were born, we were a pure being. We had no boundary other than our skin. We had no way to protect ourselves from the harsh environment. We required others to protect us or we would die.

Sometimes, that environment says anger is not accepted, that we're not important, that we must fear closeness. So we begin developing a hard outer shell like the acorn. Script can be viewed as the outer shell we originally created to protect ourselves. The seed of spirituality remains in us, and it needs protection while we're growing in strength. If the outer coating does not come off, the seed rots. It slowly dies. For a seed to continue growing, it needs to crack, to open, so it can experience the light. The seed also needs nourishment, soil, and water. It needs pruning and protection. There will be growth when it responds to its urge to grow, pushes through the hard earth, reaches for the sun, and becomes what it is, its own uniqueness.

If the spiritual seed in us lies dormant, we die. We have that inner call to grow and be, to follow our path. If we're fortunate, life will provide the opportunities that will prompt us on that path. We often need pain, as harsh as it may be, to crack our outer shell. Had our parents been wise enough, informed enough, and nourished enough themselves, they would have naturally provided these openings. Often they did not, for they could not. If life doesn't provide us with the appropriate shocks, we can be sure we will create them as we live out our life drama. Through these shocks we claim our autonomy and then reach for the transcendent. This all happens naturally, for it is our true nature.

## THE IMPORTANCE OF UNDERSTANDING THE SPIRITUAL LOVER

Know that you have all three selves in you: learned, autonomous, and spiritual. The question is, which is running your life at any one time? You may not always be expressing the self you want to be, but understanding this model can encourage you to perceive the process from your highest part—the spiritual lover. Those of you who do often have an easier time in your relationships.

What does spirituality have to do with love addiction? Everything. You can be in the middle of an argument, a trauma, a bewildering problem and step back and look at it from a spiritual perspective. Though self-integration is necessary, we don't have to be fully integrated to view life from a spiritual self or to develop our spiritual lover. Often, people describe the growth from autonomy to spirituality with the languages of religion or poetry. This is true of Kelley's story, which sums up many of the ideas I've discussed.

*Kelley's Story:* *"When I cut loose the litany of painful legacies, lights began to shine in my heart."*

Growing up, I felt like I was standing outside of life, pushing my nose against the window pane. I wanted to peer into the hearts of my friends, who I thought all fit snugly into their warm, happy, American homes.

I looked like an all-American kid: blonde hair, freckles, blue eyes, round face. I loved to climb trees and chew bubble gum. I did well in most everything.

But no one knew my secret: My parents were addicts. I pretended I was fine, but my father, a physician, was a morphine addict.

My mother, my revered goddess of strength, eventually lost contact with the old-fashioned girl in love she had been! The graceful refinery chipped away, until finally she dismissed the dream. I refused to admit to her failure. I guarded her with my life. Mother was an alcoholic.

Childhood reverence constantly commanded my private thoughts: *Exalt your loved ones before yourself.* I followed the decree. Freedom ceased to be an option.

I was only a caterpillar then. I needed my parents like little caterpillars need solid surfaces to attach all those fuzzy feet to. I never learned how to generate fuel just for myself. I never dreamed I could soar.

But it's never too late to become a butterfly. I know that now. I survived the metamorphosis of each parent before my own.

The metamorphosis didn't register at first. I only saw the addictive part: a cocoon wrapped tightly—removing them from me. I watched the pain on their faces, and I acknowledged it thoroughly time and time again.

Addicted to the picture of the addiction, I pretended I was fine.

Daddy almost died and he stopped using drugs. Mother almost died and she stopped using alcohol. Both victors. Still, I stuck stubbornly to the original view.

We each seek our own salvation. We are our own best critics, our own best judges of what is real. "Work out just our salvation with fear and trembling," it says in the Bible.

My parents survived humiliation and discord. They lived full cycle. Their metamorphosis was their business. They suffered, and then they achieved butterfly status.

The incomplete one was me. I feared finding my own separate self. A new thought came to me: *Unless I relinquish this rigid view of pain from the past, I will never let go of my own in the present.*

Suddenly I felt different. My thoughts discovered depth. They burrowed down to a place where addiction has no jurisdiction, to a beautiful place where nothing bad exists.

I've begun to shed the outside trapping of what I witnessed. With it goes an unhealthy preoccupation with pain and suffering. Beauty is becoming dear.

As I continue to adjust my sights about the human condition, I see that each of us can claim freedom. Love emerges victorious from bewildering battles of murky memories. Out of clouds come angels showing us the way to fly.

Mary Baker Eddy, founder of the Christian Science Church, says, "As human thought changes from one stage to another of conscious pain and painlessness, sorrow and joy—from fear to hope and from faith to understanding—the visible manifestation will at last be man governed by soul, not by material sense."

When I cut loose the litany of painful legacies, lights began to shine in my heart. Freedom is understanding. And there's always time left to become a butterfly.

We've learned about how we can open up to our spiritual-ity. But how does this sense of spirituality change our relationships in daily life? There is a spiritual lover in each of us. And though bringing our spiritual lover into our life is an ideal, we are challenged to recognize our spiritual lover and let it be the leading edge in our love life. This is the subject we turn to in the next chapter.

## ACTIVITY

### *The Transformational Script*

Here are questions that can help you assess your level of commit-ment to transformation. Again, take all the time you need to answer each question. You may want to take a pen or pencil and write out your answers on a separate sheet of paper.

1. What experiences continue to interfere with your birth into wholeness?
2. What are you doing to grow from these experiences?
3. Viewing relationship as a teacher, list significant relationships and what they taught you about yourself.
4. How do you attempt to fill spiritual voids? (Your answer may include fun, money, work, sex, power, drugs, excitement, addictive relationships, etcetera.)
5. How might you improve the spiritual quality of your life?
6. On a scale of 0 to 10 (10 high), how important are the following to you? To your partner? Note: If there is a wide discrepancy between your score and your partner's score, it is worth discuss-ing with each other.

- Spiritual values/needs
- Mystical experiences
- Being true to self
- Self-mastery
- Bliss, wonder
- Wise inner guide
- Spiritual lover
- Cosmic humor and playfulness
- Solitude

## CHAPTER FIVE

# *The Spiritual Lover in You*

*When love beckons to you follow him,*
*Though his ways are hard and steep.*
*And when his wings enfold you yield to him,*
*Though the sword hidden among his pinions may wound you.*
*And when he speaks to you believe in him,*
*Though his voice may shatter your dreams, as the north wind*
  *lays waste the garden.*
*For even as love crowns you so shall he crucify you. Even as he*
  *is for your growth so is he for your pruning.*
*But if in your fear you would seek only love's peace and love's*
  *pleasure,*
*Then it is better for you that you cover your nakedness and pass*
  *out of love's threshing-floor.*

— *Kahlil Gibran*

It has been said that real love hurts and that if it doesn't devastate you, it is not love. For in love you are absolutely vulnerable, open. This openness to another is so complete that there are no empty places in the soul. This love takes you far beyond yourself to the experience of union with all of life. In that union, you embrace both joy and sorrow as cohabitants of life.

## THE EMERGENCE OF THE SPIRITUAL LOVER

We have defined *love* and we have defined *power*. You have learned that you bring three lovers, not one, into each relationship.

- There is the addictive lover who is attached to itself or the love object and creates havoc in every relationship it enters.
- There is the autonomous lover, who loves in a profoundly human and committed way. Having released its fears and negative thinking, it mutually shares love and power, and meaningful partnerships then evolve.
- And there is the spiritual lover, who knows in depth the true meaning of love and power.

The more complete our love is, the more intimate we allow ourselves to be, the closer we are to our spiritual core. When that core is a part of our relationships, love defies all words. When love comes from the heart, the soul, the mind, and the body, we emerge into the spiritual lover.

Though this is a possibility, it remains an ideal toward which we continually must strive. As we own and shed the darkness in our psyche, we experience more and more moments of spiritual love in our relationships. As we begin to recognize these moments, we can lock them in our human memory bank. We can then count on returning to them again and again.

With all the pressures to be otherwise, it is difficult to sustain the spiritual lover in ourselves. Yet, bringing this lover into our relationships is perhaps the only hope we have. For it is the spiritual lover in us that can reveal previously unknown depths of love. And it is the spiritual lover in each of us that claims the intensity of our power, that inspires us to love fearlessly. We have learned that love without power goes idle; power without love injures. Love with power now becomes the answer, the living metaphor in our relationships. Once dormant, now awakened, these spiritual energies produce an intoxicating feeling of such profound magnitude that all at once we feel the best aspects of ourselves. We transcend the usual pettiness and negativity that have dominated our relationships.

### Experiencing *Amour*

Hints of recognizing the spiritual lover appeared at the beginning of the twelfth century when the concept of courtly love was introduced.[1] Passionate love for another person, rather than being deplored and sinful, was viewed as a love that came from deep in the soul. Passion meant suffering. The spiritual lover willingly accepted it. This allowed the love-inspired man and woman a nobility of character that transformed them and invited their deepest virtues. A new deference for women, the feminine, flourished. *Eros,* our longing for physical union, united with *agape,* the spiritual love of our neighbor, and became *amour,* that profound and deeply personal love relationship.

Amour, to the troubadours, became the ultimate religious experience. They claimed that the soul could be experienced in the meeting of the eyes, and in that meeting there was a recognition of mutual identity, a spiritual union. This spiritual moment preceded any physical union. The physical expression became but the sacrament that confirmed the deeper connection. This experience is in complete contrast to the lover of euphoria or the sexual addict, both of whom seek the physical sensation first; here, the soul is uninvolved, and the addictive lover remains void and empty, save for a brief moment of union that cannot be sustained. Rather than feeling virtuous and complete, self-hate, anger, disgust, disdain, numbness, and boredom become the rule.

Though there are many we can and do love, we continue to long for primary relationships that will harmonize with the spiritual essence of all of life and that yet speak to our individuality. The more awake and more conscious we become, the more likely we are to invite spiritual lovers into our life. For consciousness seeks consciousness. When this happens, there is a mystical knowing, a mystical rejoicing over the union. Just as the universe follows patterns and works toward a unified whole, so does the spiritual lover. When people belong, everything seems to fall in place, even in times of chaos and doubt. Something inside says, *This is it.*

## CHARACTERISTICS OF THE SPIRITUAL LOVER

Our spiritual lover goes one step beyond ordinary, healthy love. While healthy love feels right and is honoring, accessing our spiritual lover is ennobling and downright divine!

What does the spiritual lover look like? How does it express itself? Though the spiritual lover doesn't need to be defined (it is what it is) it's helpful to know what it looks like. Indeed, we might discover that the following characteristics describe experiences we've had but may have overlooked. Since most of our time is spent in our human conditioning, we fail to sustain our spiritual lover. Though it may not rise to the surface, it is always there in potentiality. The spiritual lover permeates and flows through all of us.

In my own work, I speak of twenty characteristics that spiritual lovers show. The spiritual lover

1. Masters the meaning of love and power.
2. Experiences sacredness in the other.
3. Fully embraces and fully expresses love.
4. Practices the wound of the heart.
5. Views love as the way out of suffering.
6. Is absolutely truthful.
7. Views itself as student and teacher.
8. Is compelled to serve the other.
9. Experiences gratitude and kindness in having been served.
10. Greets love with more love.
11. Sees sexual union as love-inspired.
12. Is luminous and radiant.
13. Dignifies the other.
14. Expresses a deep tenderness.
15. Experiences oneness and completeness.
16. Savors the moment.
17. Totally accepts the human self.
18. Resolves conflict from the heart.
19. Shares from the soul.
20. Surrenders to the laws of transformation.

## Masters the Meaning of Love and Power

Individually, spiritual lovers have not only discovered the relationship of love with power—they are living it now. The spiritual lover understands the divine relationship between the grail and the sword, the gentle and the strong, the earth and the sky, the union of matter and spirit. The inner male and inner female have married. Love with power emerges as a gentle confidence.

*Stan and Margie's Story: "Unconditional love does not need power plays."*

Tired of feeling powerless, Margie began giving more time to her own personal development. In that development, she discovered an overwhelming sense of unconditional love within herself. She discovered her own inner teacher. Needless to say, this changed the dynamics of her relationship with her partner Stan, who liked to control. Accustomed to having someone anticipate his needs and be "one down," Stan began threatening to leave the relationship. Margie replied from a place of love. She said, "I love you. How can I be with you in a way that honors us both?" Stan, remembering the deep spiritual connection he felt with Margie in the first weeks they were together, somehow managed in his humility to let his spiritual lover come forth. "I love you too," he said. "I'm confused by your changes, but I'm willing to do what we can to rebuild our relationship." What they both learned is that unconditional love does not need power plays.

## Experiences Sacredness in the Other

The spiritual lover knows that being in love can be the most powerful experience of all and senses that every moment is a miracle. Simple things become joyful—a walk in the park, a Thursday night pizza ritual. Communication is in the shared experience and not always in words. In spiritual love the silence itself becomes sacred. This is unlike the tense silence of withholding, where a wall exists to prevent intimacy. Spiritual lovers know that though the love they experience was triggered by the other person, it comes from their own sacredness—that quiet place within.

I saw this sense of sacred while watching a friend experience the death of his loved one. They had, for the most part, a good and solid relationship. Being human, of course, they occasionally disagreed and lashed out. But somehow they always transcended the disagreements. They never ended a day without renewing their love. Rather than focusing on the pain of ultimate separation, though it was often there, they focused on their strength, their dignity, and their deep love. Each moment was sacred and deeply felt. Each moment was a "forever" that saw them through the most difficult of times.

In essence their love said, *I know God because of our love.* He saw her as a sacred reflection of the universe, and in her dying she brought out the sacredness in him. And because of that sacredness, they were able in their sorrow to fully release each other—one to life, one to death. They were not attached to the bodily form of the other person. They knew their sacred intimacy would last even beyond death.

### Fully Embraces and Fully Expresses Love

Perhaps one of the greatest pains we can experience in our love relationships is that of love being rejected. It hurts deeply to not be free to give from the heart. It hurts, too, when the heart is open to another but the other cannot receive. The pain of love not being embraced produces great sorrow. The spiritual lover, having transcended the negative beliefs, fears, decisions, and addictions that kept it fearfully alone, is now free to fully embrace the love offered. The spiritual lover not only takes in but fully expresses love. Love literally saturates two lovers. Both hearts are open. Love, power, wisdom—all present themselves at once.

One person, recovering from a host of addictions including sexual addiction, cautiously shared with me that he was in a new love relationship. Was it but another substitute, he asked, another quest for self-gratification? I asked him if he was in love, and he said, "I don't know. I don't know if I would recognize it. But something about this is very, very different. I have strange feelings throughout my entire being, not just my body."

"Check to see if that feeling starts with a fullness in the heart and spreads outward," I replied. "If it does, it is likely to be love and if so, embrace it and enjoy. Now that you are sober, you are free to feel what you were not free to feel before. You may just have opened up to love."

### Practices the Wound of the Heart

Spiritual lovers practice the wound of the heart. They know love is bigger than pain and death. They aren't afraid to love so deeply, so mutually, so completely that a conflict may produce pain. And in this willingness to embrace pain they gain, as Linda and Joseph's story reveals, the means to transcend it.

*Linda and Joseph's Story: "They laid down the walls and embraced."*

> Linda and Joseph were having a tumultuous year. Linda, on one hand, was adjusting to the birth of another child and had given up her job to stay home. Intense feelings of rage and of being unimportant surfaced. Flashbacks to a childhood that lacked emotional support intensified.

> Joseph, on the other hand, was struggling to survive in a family business that provided no male mentors, only critical reviewers attempting to control his fate. Linda demanded more attention; Joseph demanded being understood. Each wanted the other to fulfill unmet needs. Both were fiercely competing to get those needs met, using usual power plays, blame, withdrawal, and self-righteous anger. Neither person felt, heard, nor truly understood the other.

> It wasn't until they transcended their competitive natures and began viewing the relationship from their spiritual lover that they discovered two things: (1) They deeply missed each other's love and spirit, and (2) they both suffered hurts not caused by the other. Because both were in need, they could not fully be there for each other. At that realization, they laid down the walls and embraced. Joy and sorrow came together in that moment.

### Views Love as the Way out of Suffering

Spiritual lovers know that pain can be transcended with love. Simply put, love calls us to task. Daily we are called to transcend our pain, our fear, our conflicts—to do hard things because we love, to do what we don't want to do because we love. The paradox is, as wide and encompassing as love is, the path of love is very narrow. Yet love can propel us into overdrive and get us through the roughest of times, as Joan's story shows.

*Joan's Story: "She saw this crisis as an opportunity."*

Joan was in great pain at the discovery that her husband was having an affair. She lost twenty pounds, was suffering despair, and was having anxiety attacks. The pain was more intense than she had experienced in her life. Familiar feelings and thoughts surfaced: *I'm not good enough. I don't deserve joy.* She questioned his trust violation and wondered whether she could get beyond it.

In the midst of her pain, she was able to gain access to her spiritual lover, remembering that this was a necessary event on a life path and need not be an end in itself. She recognized that part of the crisis was precipitated by her letting go of the old and walking more on her own spiritual path. "I stopped being a doormat, a naive rescuer, and putting him on a pedestal," said Joan. She saw this crisis as an opportunity to transform an outdated relationship to one of deeper love. In fact, this knowledge was about all she could count on some days. Though the relationship is still evolving, spiritual love is at work. The spiritual lover views problems from the top, from the highest possible level and possibility.

## Is Absolutely Truthful

Trust is the basis of love, the very foundation. The spiritual lover has integrity, is loyal, and behaves in such a way as if to say, "I am here for you." A feeling of safety is present. That absolute trust sanctifies the relationship. There are no lies, no hidden darkness. For the purity and openness of the spiritual lover cut through deceit. It is truth, it knows the truth, it speaks the truth. The spiritual lover knows when something is amiss and calls it to attention. It says, "Something is very wrong here! When we are truthful, we don't make anyone wrong." Only the behavior is wrong. Curt and Kim learned the importance of this kind of truth.

*Curt and Kim's Story:* "*Tell me the truth. Truth I can handle.*"

Curt knew something was not right and suspected Kim was having an affair with a co-worker. When he brought it to her attention, she denied it adamantly. This invited him back into denial. But for him the negative feelings were too strong. He checked into himself to see where the feeling came from—paranoia, fear, or a deeper knowing. He determined it was a deeper knowing. With that knowledge he confronted Kim and this time said, "I must trust what I know. I love you. Tell me the truth. Truth I can handle. Are you having an affair?" With that, Kim acknowledged having an emotional affair with her co-worker and was relieved to have it openly discussed. Truth led to healing.

## Views Itself as Student and Teacher

The spiritual lover experiences itself and others as emotional and spiritual equals. Each is student and each is teacher. Lovers are mirrors, reflecting back to the other. Just as each droplet of rain reflects the immense universe, so each person is a scaled down model of the great divine. Knowing this, the spiritual lover, free of criticism and fault finding, does what it can to support the other in creating personal meaning, in realizing that person's potentials. If spiritual lovers do not like what they see, they do something about it now. For they recognize that that fault in the other person is no doubt a part of themselves as well. This was true of Char.

*Char's Story:* "*With grief and joy, she let go of the relationship.*"

Char questioned why she had drawn yet another narcissistic partner into her life. It didn't make sense. She had done much of her inner work and was living what she was learning. Then "he" showed up and sparked love in her. She was challenged daily to be patient, kind, yielding, supportive of his level of awareness, one that barely surpassed addiction.

"Am I mad?" she asked herself. "Am I going backwards?" The spiritual lover in her simply said, "You are both teachers, and it won't be long for the student to show up." At the same time, she was challenged to stay with her own truth, to set her limits. She saw narcissism in herself as she struggled with wanting him to rise to her level and serve her needs. In response, he felt a spiritual tenderness and an opening of the heart that he had never before experienced. Even so, he ultimately chose to stay with his addictions. With grief and joy, she let go of the relationship as she recognized he had been her spiritual lover, thus a teacher. She had seen her own narcissistic self, which she had previously not noticed. Thus, she was the student. She recognized that both of them were the teacher and student. Having learned the lesson she was free to move on.

### Is Compelled to Serve the Other

Compelled by love, a spiritual lover experiences a deep desire to care for the other: "I love you," it says, "and therefore I am serving you." The service is simple and direct. There are no hidden motives, no strings attached, no giving to get something in return. Free of codependent urges, the serving, the offers, come from the heart. The spiritual lover says, "I am here for you." It gives of itself. There is joy in the giving, and joy is the reward. The spiritual lover experiences serving as love in action.

When we love deeply, we begin to serve naturally. The spiritual lover knows that it is not how much we give, but how much love is in the giving. To the spiritual lover, generosity is the basis of a harmonious relationship. *Give till it hurts*, the spiritual lover knows, does not mean give to enable or rescue.

### Experiences Gratitude and Kindness
### In Having Been Served

Not only does the spiritual lover desire to care for another, the spiritual lover will experience a deep sense of gratitude and kindness in response to the others who serve. Unlike the human lover who measures, who feels trapped in obligation, or undeserving and guilty, the spiritual lover fully acknowledges the gift of having been served and, in that acknowledgement, returns love. As Ann and Steve found, a fullness is experienced, and the circle of love is made complete.

*Ann and Steve's Story: "I learned the true meaning of love."*

> Ann was terminally ill. Initially she denied it and pushed to be the ideal mother and wife, refusing to ask for what she needed. At one point, her husband Steve, who was in contact with his spiritual lover, stopped and said, "Ann, I love you so very much; please let me care for you." They both dropped their denial, the limited thinking, the complaining. He cared for her from his heart. She took in that care with gratitude. She lived for two more years, and in that time, even with the possibility of death facing them each day, Ann and her husband grew in strength, wisdom, and mutual love.
>
> At the time of her death, their marriage felt complete. "It is unfortunate that we need death to knock on our door before we wake up to the possibility of just how deeply two souls can give and receive," Steve said. "It was in gracing her death by serving her that I learned the true meaning of love."

### Greets Love with More Love

Something happens when spiritual lovers love. The mutuality of the love generates even more love. That love expands and keeps on expanding. How this happens is a mystery. We only know that it does happen. Spiritual lovers have no walls or sharp edges—only a field of energy. When that energy is love, it's expansive. Every time the spiritual lover loves, that love connects to the mind and the soul of the other. This love is experienced as coming from the heart, permeating first the body and then extending outward. The love seems to saturate and have no end. It is the feeling that goes past emotions. The only way to stop it is to put up a wall. For people like Brad, the fullness of love can feel so overwhelming that they become afraid and close down for a time.

**Brad's Story:** *"The key to love was within him."*

Brad, a successful, hard-driving businessperson, knew how to generate and regenerate the dollar. He set goals and met goals. Money seemed to beget more money. Not so in love. One relationship failure followed another. No wonder: His parents had a poor relationship, and early on he was hell-bent on avoiding that mistake. Love for him was a quest, an ideal. It had to be perfect or not at all.

Brad learned that all the love he desired was within his reach now. The only thing stopping the experience was his desire to control it. An eager student, he went into the tar of his cells, emptied the gunk from his psyche, and discovered love. His first experience was total love of self that "lit his rocket." He felt more alive and vibrant than ever before.

Then came the test of opening up and sharing the experience. His learned self cautioned him, *Better be careful—remember what happened to your dad. He got close and got hurt.* In spite of the warning, he took the test. He loved, truly loved. The experience was so powerful, he said, that it was "as though the universe moved through me." He learned that the key to love was within him and that his partner, though the one he was passionately drawn to, was not the reason for his love feelings. Those feelings had always been there. Brad and his partner had to be fully open to be spiritual lovers and perceive the depth and beauty of the other.

## Sees Sexual Union as Love-Inspired

The spiritual lover knows the difference well between love and sex. Love inspires the wish for sexual fusion, and that love comes first. Spiritual lovers enter the union from the essence of their being. In its highest form, sexual union, orgasm, can be experienced in absolute stillness, with no sense of grasping or need. No movement is required or necessary. The spiritual lover opens fully. The primal energy releases at the base of the spine, uncoils upward through the heart, the mind, right out of the body, and unites with all and everything. This is true release, true orgasm. The full expression of primal sexual energy and passion opens the heart spiritually to a transcendent orgasm, out of the body and into the soul. Spiritual masters have written and spoken of this experience. Few attain it, yet it's possible. Techniques and "how tos" won't help. As Andy learned, only deep spiritual union can guarantee it.

*Andy's Story:* "*It blew me out of my socks.*"

> After his divorce, Andy had a tendency to have sexual affairs. Though many of these sexual experiences were physically satisfying, even exciting, he admitted to an emptiness, a void after each one. He had to shut off any feelings from the heart to justify his sexual encounters. When he shared his conquests with friends, he received admiration for not getting involved. He became more and more shallow, less loving, sometimes outright callous in his relationships.
>
> Eventually Andy began disliking himself. He felt alienated. "This is not what some more enlightened part of me wants," he admitted. Responding to that inner spark of knowing, he stopped the affairs. "I saw that much of what I did was to get back at women who had hurt me, and in so doing I hurt myself," he said. It took quite some time to find his heart again, and when he did, a new woman, a spiritual lover, entered his life. As he increasingly shared love from the heart, a loving friendship grew. One evening, both fully open and tenderly embracing without any expectation, he experienced total orgasm without intercourse. "It blew me out of my socks, out of my mind," he recalled. "The experience defied words."

## Is Luminous and Radiant

Spiritual lovers express a kind of radiance. With a presence that can light up a room, spiritual lovers are easy to recognize. This is the light that shines through the learned self. It is there in each of us, shaded only by the darkness of our script. The heavier the shade of the script, the dimmer the light will be. When lit, this light literally attracts other people. As Barbara and Tom discovered, once we recognize it, we notice when it is going out.

**Barbara and Tom's Story:** *"They knew when the light was out, and they missed it."*

> Barbara felt Tom closing down. It was a slow process, and she knew it was happening. Unaware he was closing down, Tom would consistently say that nothing was wrong or different. At three o'clock one morning, unable to sleep, she said, "Tom, we need to get to the truth of what's happening." It took a four-hour discussion, but they did get back to their spiritual lovers. The light went on. And it wasn't the dawn that turned on the light. Once they experienced the luminousness of the spiritual lover, they knew when the light was out, and they missed it.

### Dignifies the Other

> *A true lover cannot be degraded with any avarice. Love causes a rough and uncouth woman to be distinguished for her hand-someness; it can endow a woman with nobility of character; it blesses the proud with humility. Oh, what a wonderful thing is love, which makes a woman shine with so many virtues.*
> —*Andreas Capellanus*

A spiritual lover dignifies itself and others. It practices virtues. In this is generated a strength, a wisdom, a compassion, a directness. Inspired by the enlightened presence of the other, spiritual lovers are moved to heightened states of awareness—even in the midst of discord. Confirmation of the spiritual lover's presence is the aliveness, the movement in the relationship. Spiritual lovers are patient, kind, gentle, sensitive, humble. They are disciplined in the art of loving and do not direct the course of love.

The spiritual lover brings these attributes into everyday life, where even work becomes love made visible. The ennobling spirit inspires the words, "You are beautiful." This beauty is the soft whispering of the soul. This beauty is not changed or discarded in altercations or discord. Sharing from the heart, spiritual lovers are able to say and mean, "I love you for the truth of who you are and what you can become," as Don discovered.

**Don and Charlotte's Story:** *"They both laughed deeply from the soul."*

> Don, having learned of the spiritual lover's attributes in a lecture, went home to find Charlotte in a foul mood, banging pots and pans, complaining, and irritated by some event of the day. His usual response would be to get scared or angry, to withdraw or attack. Instead, he opened to his spiritual lover. He walked over to his partner, embraced her, looked her in the eyes, and said, "You are the most beautiful person I know." With that, she let go of her anger. They both laughed deeply from the soul.

**Expresses a Deep Tenderness**

The spiritual lover naturally affirms, cares for, and cherishes the beloved. In strength, the spiritual lover expresses a deep tenderness, a soft, gentle touch as though sacred. Spiritual lovers, having the freedom to own the best aspects of themselves, share their receptive and feminine qualities. The touch is one of gentle exploring. It is timeless, yet familiar, saying, "I see and experience the miracle in you. You are a wonder. And through you I see and experience me." This touch, as Ned and Lana found, goes beyond the affectionate, the sensual. It is the touching of two souls saying hello.

**Ned and Lana's Story:** *"Six weeks of loving touch did wonders."*

> Ned and Lana hadn't been physically intimate for months and were angry, sad, and depressed. Intimacy had different meanings for each of them. For him it was sexual; sex was his right. "If it isn't given, you take it," his father had said. For her, intimacy was a longing for affection, and as the middle child in a large family, she felt she missed out on her fair share. Both had a misguided definition of

closeness. They were encouraged to explore spiritual intimacy to free themselves to simply love via deep, caring touch. Six weeks of loving touch did wonders. No longer focused on sex or groping for affection, they experienced both naturally.

## Experiences Oneness and Completeness

Spiritual intimacy can be described as a sacred feast in the heart of God, for it is the ultimate experience of spiritual lovers. The union is so profound that there is an experience of *always was and always will be, forever and ever.* There is a deep knowing of the words, "I belong with you." In a marriage, spiritual lovers simply celebrate with witnesses what is already there. The thirst of our being for wholeness has been achieved.

The spiritual lover has moved from the certain to the uncertain to the certain again.

- *Certain*—As infants we are at one with the universe. We are *certain* of who we are.
- *Uncertain*—Having no boundary or way to defend ourselves, we begin absorbing other people's thoughts, feelings, and behaviors, becoming *uncertain* as to who we truly are—or where we stop and someone else begins.
- *Certain again*—As we claim autonomy by releasing negative influences from our psyche, we return to being *certain* of who we are. Now we are free to return to the state of no boundaries again, without fear of losing ourselves.

The spiritual lover feels at one with the universe—unity consciousness. In this union, the spiritual lover transcends its humanness and completes the circle. There are no empty spaces, no shadows present in the soul. Being with an open person, living love, the spiritual lover experiences an eternal now, unity with all of life. In the sharing of unconditional love and completeness, needs no longer exist. Nothing is lacking, and nothing needs to be attained. Rick explains this completeness.

*Rick's Story: "We . . . let go of our learned self."*

Love is not a technique, it is a shared experience. Happiness can only come through an open and willing heart. My partner and I each had to examine the wounds that prevented the heart-to-heart sharing. Reluctantly, she and I began our personal growth processes. We were amazed to discover how we had been programmed to close down, shut off, power play. Through a long process, we were able to let go of our learned self long enough to return to a deep sense of belonging and caring—a oneness.

## Savors the Moment

Because of our human conditioning, moments of bliss and spiritual loving may be the exception, not the rule. Knowing this, the spiritual lover takes stock of and savors each timeless moment and keeps them like jewels. These precious memories, never to be forgotten, are locked in the psyche. Spiritual lovers call on these moments to get them through hard times, difficult tasks, and doubt. Often, these memories are the only thing that can sustain a love relationship. Such was the situation for Mark.

*Mark's Story: "I was able to release my fearful memories."*

In an angry moment my partner threatened to leave. Memories of three failed relationships began to scare me. When my partner and I met, our spiritual lovers were active and present. Two things we had discussed and agreed upon were, one, to cherish and express appreciation for the gift of our love and, two, to never forget the special moments, to know that these are what count and what our love is really about. I was able to release my fearful memories and return once more to my spiritual lover.

## Totally Accepts the Human Self

Recognizing the importance of its human needs, the spiritual lover never denies or ignores them. Instead, the spiritual lover works through the human self and is totally accepting of it. This is important to understand. Though the spiritual lover knows the human self from another reality, it creates a partnership with both learned and autonomous selves.

This partnership allows for the full expression of all of our primal energy, the best aspects of being human. It also recognizes when it is important to let the human run the show, when spirituality has become too much, when we have become too understanding, too compassionate, too giving, to the demise of the inner child. Too much can get us back into rescuing, enabling, and codependency, where both spirit and inner child die. When we've stopped listening to our inner teacher and speaking our own truth, our spiritual lover will recognize when enough is enough. The spiritual lover knows the human may need to make messes to learn more lessons to develop more spirituality, and it allows for this. It is not spiritual versus human lover; it is living with both. The spiritual lover appreciates and lives fully in the body. It appreciates and takes in the material world. It knows that if we were meant to be angels we'd be angels, and we are not. It knows the down-to-earth living that allows for spiritual experiences, realizing that we are really spiritual lovers having human relationships.

The spiritual lover knows that love has cycles and seasons. At times in our relationships, we are required to spend more time in the material world—the world of work, money, and interpersonal conflict. And yet if we idle there, we begin losing touch with the spiritual lover, and we can gently pull ourselves back on track. This balance is a delicate and necessary one.

Theresa described it the following way.

**Theresa's Story:** *"Sharing of work . . . makes more room for . . . flights with our spiritual lovers."*

Owning my spiritual lover is an important part of my love relationship. I savor the moments it is present. It is the foundation of the relationship I'm in. My partner and I experience a multitude of relationships. We are friends, mentors, and we have taken on the awesome task of running a business together. A whole new arena has opened.

The material world is on us in full force. Our time and attention has been redirected. Linear thinking, structure, planning, and long hours are required. And though we know that it is all necessary and temporary and that we have mutually agreed to it, there comes a point where we find it crossing the line and detracting from the spiritual lover in each of us. Though we can see how the material and spiritual are both necessary, we are in new territory together and struggling for the balance. Sometimes, we don't come back to earth at the same time.

The image that comes to me is that of our spiritual lovers flying high, having a great time. The material world calls and says, "It's time to get your feet on the ground. There are important things to do at work." But my partner keeps flying and on occasion comes down to touch base and check in. Feeling stuck in the material plane and often feeling overloaded, I call out, "Get down here, the load's too heavy." He doesn't like the shouting and just keeps flying. When I stop shouting and simply do what I can do, he looks down, sees the distance, recalls what he has agreed to do, and joins me. Working together in the material world is rewarding. Mostly though, the sharing of work tasks makes more room for joint flights with our spiritual lovers.

## Resolves Conflict from the Heart

*The answer to all problems, fear, and pain, the strong victor over death, is love.*

—*White Eagle*

The spiritual lover is a warrior and not afraid to stand up for its truth. Love is a sword it uses in conflict. Where it cuts it gives life, not death. The spiritual lover excels in using love with power to resolve problems. There is a spiritual commitment to get through ordeals and hard times. Discord, disagreement, and confrontation are resolved from the heart.

The spiritual lover recognizes that there is a shadow in each of us, that the spirit goes wandering off, that we commit wrong and that the wrong must be confronted if a relationship is to heal and grow. When wrongdoing is confronted from the heart, lovers can still feel good and secure. Forgiveness is inherent in the experience. When this is lacking, a person can feel tired, mean, insecure, separate.

A warrior comes to grips with problems in everyday living in practical and loving ways. The spiritual lover recognizes that everyday contact with ordinary people is our spiritual school and that we are students. We are required to stay and face the unpleasant. No one can run from life experiences. The challenge is to bring love to bear on them.

The spiritual lover is able to gaze right to the core of other people and see that they have heart and soul. The spiritual lover sees that those people are not their behavior. Weaknesses, faults, labels, judgments, and criticism are replaced with love for who each person is and can yet become. Where there is love there is the possibility of a miracle. Conflict, confrontation with the spiritual lover in charge, will lead to growth. No matter how deep the hurt, how bitter the words, spiritual love can erase it. The inflictor can desire to stop the hurt; the receiver can desire to forgive. Conflict can be viewed as one of the complications, one of the tests of love, as it was for Barbara and Tom.

***Barbara and Tom's Story:*** *"The conflict changed into a deeper love and respect."*

> Tom and I had reached a dead end in an argument. I saw no way out of our dilemma. I did not feel Tom even heard me. In my desperation I lashed out and said, "I want you to leave." Tom turned, looked directly into my eyes, and spoke firmly from his heart: "No, I will not go. I love you. I have committed to staying." The look penetrated my heart. It motivated me to let go of the self-righteous anger and discover that the real feeling was sorrow for the lost affection in our relationship. I missed Tom. With the discovery, we were able to have a heart-to-heart talk. The conflict changed into a deeper love and respect. Tom had stayed separate from my demand for him to leave—no easy job.

**Shares from the Soul**

Some say love is only possible if two persons touch each other's souls. I once heard that if in six months into a relationship the spiritual lovers don't meet and jell, the relationship will not make it. No soul, no go! Couples who are right for each other find communication easy. Sometimes there is no need to even talk, the feeling of sharing is so strong. The words "I love you" are redundant, a confirmation that the human self simply likes to hear. Spiritual lovers often communicate telepathically. That is, they know when they are needed, and they sense the other's presence over great distance.

Spiritual lovers experience a comfort in the closeness and stillness. Tension and uneasiness are not present. There may well have been an uneasiness, a tension when the human lovers first met. They may have even fought the inevitable because it didn't fit their plans. It may have defied the rules of systems. It may have not seemed to make any sense. Or perhaps because of their deep knowing that they belong together the human part of them wasn't ready for it yet.

As we've learned, the learned self often selects relationships to fit its negative beliefs. When it encounters someone who can share from the soul, it often doesn't know what to do. To spiritual lovers, there is no hit or miss in a relationship. The universe arranges this one. Spiritual lovers release all expectations, control, and simply get ready for each other. When spiritual lovers meet, the tie can never be broken by them or anyone else. The bond may weaken, they may even separate, but that bond will be permanent. There is yet another element to this sharing—when spiritual lovers touch, there is a healing that is physical, mental, emotional, spiritual.

This often means staying open to a new relationship even if the time is not "right." It can also mean patiently waiting for the other person to open up.

**Surrenders to the Laws of Transformation**

Living the life of a spiritual lover, following the path of the heart, means getting the ego out of the way. It means that we stop measuring and controlling our love life. The spiritual lover recognizes that loving is natural to us and that the universe has provided principles and laws to guide its unfolding. The spiritual lover, in tune with these laws, opens itself to the constant possibility that every moment of a relationship can be graced. In this regard, grace becomes the experience of embracing and giving love. Spiritual lovers, in tune with the laws and principles, know a profound mystical intimacy where love and power merge. Working with these laws is so important that we will examine them more fully in the next chapter as a guiding force in the process of healthy love.

## YOUR SPIRITUAL LOVER IS ALWAYS PRESENT

The spiritual lover is always there. It can be active or it can be latent and blocked. It is like a light always burning, only shadowed by our traumas of omission and commission, our history, our cultural roles, our personal scripts, and perhaps even our religious beliefs.

If you haven't experienced the spiritual lover, you might not miss it. Once you have experienced it, however, you will surely know when it's gone. And when it's veiled is when you come out loud and clear and say with conviction from the heart, "Something's very wrong here."

The spiritual lover never has to be reminded of the ways it manifests. It knows them well. It's our learned self that needs the list of characteristics we've just surveyed. We can let these characteristics be guideposts to help us recognize when we're on or off the path. Perhaps they can help us mark our progress, for we seem to be much more mindful of our human than spiritual lovers. You may remember many times when your spiritual lover was captain of your ship. Savor these moments. They are real and vital. As one woman said, "Knowing these moments has helped me rise above many difficulties in my relationship."

Sometimes, the spiritual lover is so powerful we get frightened and move away. How often have we said, "That person is so good, I'm uncomfortable around her"? Often, good people are abused, negated, or made unimportant in our life. At times, the hectic pace of life numbs our spiritual lover.

As we have seen, it is a daily struggle for the learned self to get beyond the constraints imposed upon us. When we review all the influences that have contributed to misguided definitions of love and power, is it any wonder the spiritual lover in each of us is lost or buried?

We must claim the light of spiritual love, live that light, and bring that light to ourselves and others—our families, our friends, and the earth. As a spiritual lover, when we transform our love into power and power into love, we are not a saint or a mystic. We live in the ranks of the ordinary. We may come in all sizes and shapes. We may be men or women. Religion doesn't automatically create us, nor are we exclusive to one religion.

The spiritual lover is present in

- the man who cares for his invalid wife.
- the woman who accepts her partner's gripes and complaints and continues to see his worth, his dignity.
- the person who speaks up for her truth and risks her partner leaving.
- the man who speaks to other men about the atrocities that have occurred when their power was without love.
- the woman who speaks to other women, urging them to look into themselves and heal the wounds and the beliefs that keep them from bringing power into love.

This is my possibility, and it is yours too.

## ACTIVITIES

### 1. Recognizing the Spiritual Lover

Ask yourself, *What do I look like when I'm a spiritual lover?* The spiritual lover is in each of us. As you have learned, it often gets lost in the shuffle of life. Its light grows dim. For some, identifying and turning on the light of the spiritual lover has had tremendous healing effects on relationships.

A list of ways you can recognize the spiritual lover appears on page 118. Review the list and indicate the percentage of time you express these in your love relationships. Again, be honest. Take this one relationship at a time, and evaluate the *relationship* itself. You may want to do an assessment for each relationship. Use a separate sheet of paper for each relationship, or make photocopies of this list if that is more convenient.

### 2. *Expanding Love*

The next exercise can be an excellent follow-up to the releasing of pain, hurt, anger you might have felt about a friend, partner, parent, or even one you consider your enemy. In that regard, when ready to forgive, the fullness of love becomes the expression of forgiveness. As you feel the fullness of love for another, your heart heals too.

Go inward and experience your heart as strong, full, healthy. Create a feeling of deep love, warmth, caring, and compassion. Image the love as a soft, flowing pink aura coming from and surrounding the heart. Let the aura extend throughout your body until it completely surrounds you. Visualize clearly the person or persons to whom you wish to direct your love. Concentrate on sending the love in the form of a soft pink cloud and see the cloud surrounding the love object. If healing is necessary, see the love providing healing protection. Without any thought of expected outcomes, let go. Trust you have done your part to share your spiritual lover.

## CHAPTER SIX

# Laws of Transformation

*The first answer to the question "what is psychology?" should be that psychology is a study of the principles, laws and facts of man's possible evolution.*

*— P. D. Ouspensky*

Transforming our love life need not be an arduous task. For, indeed, if we get the ego out of the way and stop attempting to control the change or becoming emotionally attached to our transformation, we will discover that the universe has provided all that we need. Principles and laws guide this transformation. By working with them, the process of love unfolds naturally.

The process of love takes place according to these laws. Though these laws have existed far longer than you and me, in our ignorance and arrogance we have had a propensity to disregard or fight them. In this blatant disregard, we make our messes and create needless suffering in our relationships. Addictive love, compulsive behaviors, and power plays are an attempt to infringe upon these universal principles as we struggle to fill the inner discontent, to search for the missing something or someone. The discontent will never be soothed by an addictive process for, as we have seen, addiction misses the point: We have not yet discovered ourselves.

The antithesis of addiction, we find, is the dynamic process of personal transformation: becoming the truth of who we really are. In this process, desire takes on a different meaning. Once, the desire to gratify the ego ruled our life; now, the guiding principle becomes following the path of the heart. We come to know the spiritual lover. We discover our capacity to relate to others and the world at a deeper level.

Let's review some of these laws. Living in tune with these laws, we open our love relationships to constant possibility. Every moment becomes a potential for good. Every moment involves spirituality. Every moment has the possibility to be graced by being fully experienced. These laws allow for a profound and mystical intimacy where love and power merge.

The universal laws that guide us are neutral, meaning that they continue to operate whether we acknowledge them or not. Let's review these laws:

- Law of Change/Transcendence
- Law of Polar Opposites
- Law of Love
- Law of Motion
- Law of Energy
- Law of Relationships
- Law of Free Will
- Law of Attraction[1]

**Law of Change/Transcendence**

Because a relationship is fluid and open-ended, all human experiences are opportunities from which to grow individually and together. We recognize that, given our life experiences, the place we're at is the only place we can be at the moment.

This law recognizes different levels of development. It states quite clearly that you can only be where you are at, and you cannot move from this place until you fully accept it. Once you do accept it, however, you are no longer there. You are a step above, looking back.

So often a person will say to me, "I don't like who or where I am, and I won't accept myself until I reach my goals." My answer is, "Then you'll probably not get there." We can move to a higher level of consciousness only after having allowed ourselves to be fully present in the pain, confusion, or unhealthy love relationship. For it is here that we learn our lessons.

We bring our uniqueness to each relationship. We are student and teacher to each other. There is no need to push or to pull ourselves or others—only to invite, encourage, step back, and watch. Sometimes we push to change faster, or we fear that we are falling behind. In these moments, we can take an eagle's-eye view of ourselves and others and see our unlimited potential and perfection. Then, we can experience the total acceptance of what is. We can encourage, inform, model, and provide opportunities that challenge or invite growth. We "light the way," so to speak. Yet, each of us will create our own dance.

As difficult a task as this is, we must be patient and willing to yield. What can help is to remember that as we transform our relationships, so will we transform our understanding. Ideas that seem incomprehensible at first will become intelligible as we change.

Tell many of us, for example, that jealousy is not a sign of love, and we will balk. But as we gradually let go of our attachments and stop seeking to possess those we love, we discover the harm in jealousy. We can look back on the times we felt jealous and realize that this emotion was simply unnecessary. Yet, we cannot expect other people still struggling with jealousy to fully accept this idea.

A person on a higher level can understand a person on a lower level because she or he has been there, just as a five-year-old can understand the world of a three-year-old. But a three-year-old cannot yet understand what it's like to be five. This law has dimensions that are hard to put in words. In some spiritual traditions, we find cryptic sayings that express it: The above contains the below and knows it; the below contains and does not yet know that which is above it. The new contains the old.

Ken is one of the people trying to understand this.

*Ken's Story:* "*When I'm in balance with myself, it's really easy just to be where I am.*"

> This law is scary in one sense, and comforting too. There is safety and integrity here. There are no expectations of perfection; it's an evolution, an evolving experience. I can simply be where I'm at, and that is really liberating for me. I can see that what I'm doing is what I've needed to do all along. It's self-honoring. Sometimes I think of myself as behind, klutzy, and I fear doing my partner's dance. I appreciate the encouragement, and yet I have to do the

process my way. I need to do my own dance. The fear comes from knowing that I'm letting go of the familiar and not knowing where I'm going. There is no map for this territory. But when I'm in balance with myself, it's really easy just to be where I am.

## Law of Polar Opposites

We tend to view life in dualities; for example, black/white, good/evil, either/or. Rather than viewing these as separate entities, the law of polarities states that opposites are two phases of the same process—flip sides of the same coin. Every positive has a potential for a negative, and each negative has the opportunity for a positive. If the opposites separate, they lose their meaning. In our either/or thinking, one aspect usually dominates, and we fail to see the whole picture. But when we're open to this law, we see things differently. We begin to realize conditions in our relationships that seem to be working against us will eventually be exactly what we need to move us to the next level.

We've already talked about several examples of this law. To know the divine world, we must understand the material world. To experience our sacred nature, we must acknowledge our inherent violence as well. Death gives birth to life, and life becomes death. Our addictive lover teaches us about spiritual love. To know the heights of joy, we need to go into the depths of pain and sorrow. To have faith, we need the experience of total doubt and cynicism. To know power, we must experience the feeling of powerlessness. It is only through the experience of our polar opposites that we become unified. For example, a person who continually says no must practice saying yes, for it is only then she or he is free to say no.

In relationships, the old teacher shows up to test us. And it may show up several times. If, like Kurt, we consistently experience the relationship from our polar opposite, our spiritual lover, we will have learned the lesson and the teacher need not return.

*Kurt's Story: "I experienced the polar opposite."*

I had worked hard for a year on letting go of an addictive relationship and preparing myself for healthy love. In that year, I had discovered myself and learned to love myself for the first time. A new person came into my life and then quickly left. *Why isn't the love of my life here yet?* I asked myself. *I've done all the right things.*

I was surprised when someone suggested that I was exactly where I needed to be and was going through a necessary part of my process. Before, when people left me I went through the experience without self-love and with negative beliefs, thinking, *I don't deserve love.* In experiencing the polar opposite, my challenge was to remain in self-love and in the knowledge that I deserved love—even when someone left me. Once I experienced the teacher from the polar opposite, I was in balance.

## Law of Love

*Love* is total expansion—reaching out from the heart, soul, body, mind, and spirit. *Contraction* is the withholding and blocking of love, erecting a wall. The law of love views us all as emotional and spiritual equals. In the law of love we no longer search for love: We are the experience of love and are free to express it in its fullness. We are already a spiritual lover.

In relationships where this is experienced, there is a synergy, a oneness. Love goes beyond merging self and others and becomes a love of life, a love of truth, and a love of God or the divine. Love embraces us as we are and separates who we are from what we feel, think, do, and choose. In love, we are one in spirit; in fear, we remain separate. The law of love requires that we look into our conditioning for all that blocks us from loving.

*Once free to love, you will have done all that is necessary in this life.*

If everyone did personal work that freed them to love, every act in the world would be an extension of our spiritual lover. Love naturally transforms and invites people to be who they are; nothing is added, only released.

Without the experience of love we are not fully alive. We merely exist. In our contracted state, we have walls. We fail to experience the meaning of the moment, the meaning in another, the meaning of life.

In the following story, Debbie speaks of how the law of love operated in her life.

***Debbie's Story:*** *"It was in them [my scars] that I found peace."*

> I once heard that a person needs to see the dark side to know the light, that within the darkness is contained the light.
>
> Several years ago, I felt desperate in a marriage I was supposed to feel good about. I was empty and searching for *something* to fill the void. Food was one thing I had control over, and it made me feel good when these bad feelings crept up. Bulimia became the darkness for me. For years, it distracted me from my life purpose.
>
> At one point I asked myself, *What am I searching for?* The answer came: happiness and peace. Then I asked, *How does one get this happiness or peace?* It came to me: through loving myself.
>
> Love of self is hard to describe. I had anticipated it to feel happy. Not so. Often it feels neutral, like a place of peace, calm, serenity, stillness.
>
> Part of getting to self-love was getting to self-forgiveness. When I forgave myself for self-abuse, I realized that I had been suppressing myself—no one had suppressed me.
>
> My husband had hurt me deeply. I had to confront the barrier that I had erected in order to survive. To be free I had to take it down. When I did, the truth of who I was, total love, was staring right at me. I became aware of my awesomeness. I regained something I thought I had lost: my power. I felt the power of the source I came from. I felt like an eagle soaring in the winds of my soul.
>
> I am both separate from and a part of my marriage. I am both separate from and a part of the God-essence. I am both separate and a part of the wholeness I experience in all of life.

This connects me to a vision of understanding that the Trinity is in each of us: Spirit—our spiritual power; Son—our humanness; Father—our soul, our home steeped in love. Essence is a combination of all three.

The painful situation with my husband has given me the opportunity to release limiting patterns and become awake to who I am.

I have always known a deep truth inside. Now it can reflect through. My outside world is a reflection of the inner. There is great wisdom in the process of life. I look at fear, and it is an illusion, it is empty. When I gave up the fear of abandonment, I set myself free.

I give thanks for my scars, for it was in them that I found peace I was looking for—love of self, love of others, love of life.

## Law of Motion

Sometimes we cling to sameness, to the predictable and the illusion of nonchange. In reality we are in motion. Life is movement, and there is no way to stop, try as we may. We are either moving forward or backward—evolution or devolution. Both of these movements are necessary. Disintegration of the old is the necessary fertilizer for the new. Leaves become the compost that feeds new life. Life is seasons, cycles, phases, and we must be willing to move through them all.

This teeming life is part of us at every level, even down to the very cells of our body. Physicists have discovered that all particles react to confinement with motion. Every particle, including those that are subatomic, can be understood only in terms of movement and inter-action, for matter is always restless and transforming. Thus, any of us who fight change in ourselves or in our relationships defies the law. Stability consists of dynamic balance.

How many times have you felt confined in your life, in your love relationships? And what is the motion you've taken to counter that confinement? The good news of this law is that pain is temporary. If you're willing to let go of it, you move with the law of motion. As you cling to pain you defy the law, and you can be sure the pain in your love life will intensify.

At times this law acts as our teacher and bids us to let go of a relationship, to go on with our life. This was what Ann expressed in a letter to her partner:

> This is a farewell letter, and I feel much grief in writing it. I have come to accept that we are in different places in terms of our love. My love for you is a deep kind of soul love, whereas you've told me that yours is not. I release you . . . gently . . . and with love. It's too painful for me to stay. To stay I'd have to numb out feelings. I'm no longer willing to do that. I believe I've done everything I can to show my love and caring for you . . . and the circle of love isn't complete. Now, I choose to let go and get on with my life.
>
> Before I leave, I want to thank you for the gifts I received in our relationship. Most importantly, I learned to accept differences rather than attempt to change them, and, when differences become too painful, to let go. I also learned what the essence of love is. It's not bearing a child or having a marriage contract. It's being open to growing in love and completing the circle in a spiritual sense. I will settle for nothing less.

## Law of Energy

The law of motion is closely related to the law of energy: All mass is energy waiting to be transformed. That includes you.

Energy is the power to live out our meaning, whether it be in a flower or a person. As human beings we are energy systems. That energy can be used to create our life and our meaning. But when energy is blocked, we implode with illness, sickness, and depression, or we explode with uncontrolled words and actions. Such is the case in addictive love, where we block our power, our life energy. We must use the energy to meet our needs and the needs of others. Compulsive behaviors are misguided ways to release this creative life force.

## Law of Relationships

*Perhaps the most fundamental law is that we are all related.* The universe is not a machine but a harmonious whole. We have no meaning as isolated entities and can only be understood in the context of our relationships. Separate, we are one thing; related, we are something entirely different. Thus, what we do with love and power *does have* an impact on others.

All entities in the universe, from molecules to nations, are integrated structures that consist of both parts and wholes. British writer Arthur Koestler calls them "holons."[2] Each holon has two complementary and yet opposite tendencies: to perform its own function and to serve a larger purpose. We can see an example in our own body. Each organ—heart, liver, lungs, kidneys—has a separate function. Yet, each is part of a larger system designed to sustain life.

In healthy love, two distinct and separate persons, the "I" and the "You," come together in a relationship that is unique in itself, a "We." Each person is then a holon that must assert its individuality, yet be willing to yield and live cooperatively within a larger relationship, the "We." This dynamic interplay assures both flexibility and openness necessary for all of life. Everywhere there is a delicate balance between integration (belonging) and self-assertion (autonomy).

In physics, the law of relationships states that all systems must balance individuality and community in an orderly way. Addictive love defies that law as it applies to our behavior: Individuality is expressed at the expense of the relationship, or personal identity is lost as the relationship becomes all-consuming. In addictive love, the relationship defines the individuals as dependent or antidependent. The system goes out of balance, withers and dies.

Mature love has unity consciousness. It encourages the growth of the individuals and simultaneously commits to the evolution of the relationship itself. Thus, the whole is and is always becoming more than the sum of its parts.

One implication of this law is that we cannot avoid *relationships.* Merely by being alive, we are related. Relationships are our destiny.

Some people, however, want to defy this law, and often early experiences play a key role in this. Keith looked into his childhood to discover why his learned self was so fearful of stepping into relationships.

**Keith's Story:** *"I got burned on my feet and in my heart."*

> I was three years old. I woke up in the middle of the night, cold and scared. I needed my mom—comfort and warmth. So I went to her room. On the way, stumbling through the dark, I stepped on a hot grill covering a heat duct. I let out a holler! My dad, who I barely knew because he had just come back from the war, greeted me with a booming voice, scolded me for interrupting *them*, and tossed me into my room like I was a nuisance. I got burned on my feet and in my heart. I decided to stop reaching out, especially to Mom.

Keith thought he could get back into his dad's and mom's good graces by not bothering them anymore. In essence, he was trying to defy the law of relationships. He'd grow up, stop needing things, and stay out of the way. His *I don't need comfort* message carried into his adult years, where it successfully masked his inner fear: Reaching out, he believed, meant getting "burned." True intimacy was avoided.

This man as a child had done his part to reach out for adult contact, as all children do. Even in our adult relationships we reach out, get burned, and resort to withdrawing, erecting walls, controlling, and telling ourselves to never foolishly trust again. The law of relationships reminds us that this is a futile quest.

**Law of Free Will**

Growth is optional. Not all will choose it. Growth means becoming more of who we already are, not what others want us to be. Growth means evolving and waking up, not remaining asleep in the illusions of the learned self.

We experience tension, a signal that it's time to grow. We also experience resistance to change. We contain these polar opposites, these co-realities. We strive for serenity, an absence of tension. Yet, a transformer knows that tension is a part of our normal movement. This tension may come in our relationships and our job, and as we view what's happening in the world. Daily, we are called to respond to the urge to grow or to choose to not respond. Not responding requires intensifying our denial, our illusions, our addictions. But responding carries the potential for us to become spiritual lovers, even when we do not understand where we are going. What we do is up to us.

### Law of Attraction

This law espouses a fundamental truth based on the theory of "100 percent intent ratio": We have in our life what we intend to have. What we don't have, we never intended, psychologically speaking. Note that this does not include times we are made victims by events beyond our control—incest, rape, war, floods, and major illness.

We are likely to attract to us that which fits our inner images. Our level of consciousness deeply influences both the people and events that come our way. For example, if a man has a healthy inner mother, he's more likely to attract an emotionally healthy woman. If his inner mother is manipulative, he may attract a manipulative woman instead. This is true for women and their inner fathers as well.

This law tells us just how important it is to create the healthy inner man and woman in us. As we do, we attract men and women who more closely fit the ideal.

If you attract a worthy person and yet reject that relationship, you are not ready for what you say you want. When you attract an unworthy person, look within.

## STAGES TOWARD TRANSFORMATION

*All things are accomplished in six stages, and the seventh brings return.*

*—From the* I Ching

The mystery of wholeness is our pilgrimage, our journey, and in that journey we don't discard. We transform and transcend. We cannot talk spirit until we fully own our inner discontent.

As we open ourselves to the laws of transformation, we find there are seven stages that naturally unfold. I conceptualized this model as I reflected upon my own journey and the journeys of those I worked with. Knowledge of the transformational stages can be helpful in recognizing where you are at in any given moment. Remember that this process is not a straight line. And, speaking holistically, we are in all stages, and all stages are related. One thing is certain, however: We do not skip stages; rather, we move through them in an orderly way, whether it be in moments or in years.

### Stage One: Denial
In denial, we operate primarily out of our life plan, our learned self. Love relationships are primarily addictive, codependent, immature. Power is out of balance. We work hard to defend our life of illusion. We look normal. Our addictions, roles, and compulsive habits keep us in our illusion. We rationalize, intellectualize. We may have religion, but not spirituality. We may deny spirituality as important or view it as shallow: "I'll pray in case there is a heaven or hell." We concretize outside events. We remain rigid, self-righteous, mechanical. We agree to competitive religious systems. We do anything and everything to keep from being awake, including walking in our sleep.

### Stage Two: Discomfort
Because our human psyche contains the seed of our essential nature, we begin to experience inner rumblings, discontent. Agitation makes denial impossible. Addictions and codependency don't work very well. Love relationships fail to give the same meaning. External world possessions, pretensions, and roles all fall short of the mark. Our real and spiritual selves want out! We may not be ready, and then we desperately cling to the familiar. We might get further enmeshed in addictions, compulsive behaviors, or unhealthy relationships. Or, listening to the inner call, we move ahead. We might have the courage to seek help. Without a shock, trauma, major problem, we may get stuck or go back to denial.

**Stage Three: Confrontation**

Our desire to grow is acknowledged. Life may have knocked on our door with a gift of pain that shakes us out of the illusion and raises our consciousness long enough to see. That major life event may be a depression, separation, rape, death, accident, chemical dependency treatment, a book, a caring confrontation, or the wisdom of age. It doesn't matter. What does matter is that we listen. Still experiencing life primarily from our learned self, we tend at first to blame other people and institutions for our discontent and stagnation, for being held back. This stage is characterized by crisis. Power plays escalate. We may even leave relationships prematurely, fight systems, drop out of society, stop going to our regular church, seek a guru, go back to discomfort and denial. Or listening to the inner urge, we may move forward and comfort our self.

With trepidation and fear, we stop! We stop looking outward to satisfy our human hunger for security, sensation, power, identity, a sense of belonging and meaning. We stop tranquilizing pain with anger, projection, willpower, compulsive behaviors, or seeking comfort in the arms of another. We stop and face our fear. We find moments of stillness in the chaos. We surrender. We humble ourselves. We feel a void and distance from others. We don't know where we're going or who will be there as we go on. We respond to the inner urge to be all that we can be.

In *Alice in Wonderland*, Lewis Carroll wrote of something much like this stage:

> I wonder if I've been changed in the night? Let me think; was I the same when I got up this morning? I almost think that I can remember feeling a little different. But if I'm not the same, the next question is "Who in the world am I? Ah, that's the great puzzle!

**Stage Four: Psychological Separation**

This is the time of self-knowledge; to explore questions: Who am I? How did I get here? Why do I do the things I do? What do I believe about love, power, men, women? What does it mean to be human?

This is a time of spiritual cleansing, getting rid of the glut and clutter we've accumulated over the years. This is a time of death—the death of the psyche as we have known it.

We own our life of illusion and take full responsibility for pain. We embrace pain as a teacher. We commit to growing. We do the inward journey to discover our real self. We experience inner conflict, discontent, fragmentation as we dialogue with figures from our unconscious that were previously denied. Sometimes we are swept off balance by these primal forces as they seek expression, heedless of the effect they have on others. It can be a painful time where we experience the dying of the old and giving birth to the new. We need faith, hope, and a lot of support from others to go into the darkness of self. We face fear with the conviction of warriorship, through we're not yet warriors. We may cling to old ways as we go into the past and heal the wounds of the traumas inflicted upon our inner child. We ask the inner child to reconsider decisions that were made that now block us from rich life experiences. We learn the difference between alone and lonely. Sometimes we feel both. We struggle to not go back to old ways. We feel separate. Not knowing or being too blocked to know who "me" is, we continue the search. We still control our addictions and negative behaviors to keep them at bay, but we have made the shift from an outer world to an inner world. We begin looking into our soul to see what effect the demons have had on us. We begin unveiling our spiritual lover that will allow us to open more fully to love and power.

### Stage Five: Resolution of Self

Something significant has happened. We have found the real "me." We are no longer trying to be a warrior. We are warriors. We have brought an ethics into our process. Our conduct, like raw instincts, is consistent with our deepest values; archetypes are tempered with love and a sense of responsibility. It is no longer a search for the self. We are ourselves. We synthesize, we blend the best aspects of human nature to form a strong, integrated personality that serves as a vehicle to express our spiritual essence. We have sorted out and kept the best aspects of our conditioning that now serve us rather than stop us. We have let go of what is no longer useful. We have thanked the learned self for what it has done for us. We experience an awakening. We recognize the three lovers in our relationships. We allow ourselves to do what we need to do and trust we will learn lessons. We commit to remaining open, even when it is painful. Transformation is now a way of life and no longer a something to somewhere.

With the heart open, we begin experiencing profound love for self that extends to others. Personality is demoted. Essence, the authentic, reigns. We transform addictions and experience natural highs, wonder, and bliss. We develop a noetic quality, we make decisions from inner knowing, and we ask deeper questions.

## Stage Six: Healthy Belonging

We're committed to bringing the spiritual lover into all of life and relationships. We feel compelled to experience the essence of others and no longer fear loss of self as we bond with another person. Challenged to live our truth, we acknowledge all the messes we create in love and in life. We are different from others, not better. We experience the desire to merge with something greater than self. We no longer need faith; we are faith. We recognize and appreciate the human self and care for it daily. Consciously we let go of addictions, compulsive behaviors, roles, and pretensions in response to a deep existential urge. Materialism is not seen as bad, but as half the truth. The process of becoming is our revolutionary task. We no longer need love, for we are the experience of love. We recognize how our inner life determines our outer experience. We love others freely and stay out of the melodrama. We power share. We recognize the best thing we can do in relationships is simply be who we are and make choices from here. Our boundary is knowing who we are and presenting that confidently to the world. We recognize that we are somebody else's mirror, and someone else is our mirror. In love we are all one. Acknowledging the three lovers we bring into relationships, we work toward harmony and profound intimacy.

If in our relationships we feel needy, we acknowledge it as simply the ego's attempt to tell us of an unmet need that is seeking expression. We develop compassionate understanding of our self and others. We resolve relationship problems from our spiritual lover.

## Stage Seven: Reaching Out

> *A teacher of God is anyone who chooses to be one.*
> —*A Course in Miracles*

Experiencing our spiritual authenticity, and committed to living from our spiritual lover, we're called to experience our uniqueness in all arenas of life. We now know the true meaning of being in the world and not of the world. We contribute, we serve from the inside. We've learned that though it may be easy to be spiritual alone on top of the mountain, our challenge is to maintain it on a daily basis. We are confronted each day to be spiritual lovers as we deal with love relationships, children, crowded freeways, money, and work relationships. And as we learn this, we teach what we know, not to change anyone, but because we recognize teacher and learner are flip sides of the same coin. The material and spiritual worlds are now required to live in harmony. This is nowhere more apparent than in living the process of healthy love, the subject of our next chapter.

## CHAPTER SEVEN

# *Love as a Process*

*We must be willing to let our relationships reveal themselves to us. If we tune into ourselves, trust ourselves, and express ourselves fully and honestly with each other, the relationship will unfold in its own unique and fascinating way.*
— *Shakti Gawain*

No one has the perfect love relationship. Love is not about perfection. Chances are relationships are spiritually nourishing, at best, 5 percent of the time. Often they run in neutral as we go about our daily business, doing the necessary tasks this earthly life requires. Often relationships are addictive as we struggle and compete for love. Perhaps the best we can hope for is to use that 5 percent when it is most needed—in the midst of relationship crisis when we need to rise above the drama, get an eagle's-eye view, and let the spiritual lover take care of business. We can, if we choose, bring consciousness into everything we do, including our love life.

## LOVE IS ALIVE

Why is it that it seems easier to feel serene on a mountain or in a meditation communing with nature than it is in our love life? Why is it so hard to be a spiritual lover? Perhaps it's because when we're on top of a mountain or enjoying nature, the privacy of our soul is pure, in tune, conscious. But because of our conditioning, a cloud covers our divinity and we see the imperfect, the negative. We find it difficult to see the royal person in ourselves and in others. Perhaps in our own darkness, our imperfection, we feel uncomfortable and undeserving.

Our compulsive human need for perfection generates the question: What is an ideal love relationship? Our compulsive need to hurry up generates the question: How can I get there now? One answer is that ideal healthy love is a *living process*. It exhibits the characteristics of life: vitality, change, evolution, animation, vigor, movement, energy, and inherent power. As a process, it advances forward, though at times it may appear to stagnate. It is ongoing. It never stops. It is fluid. It does not concern itself with content, outcomes, or form, for it is continually becoming something different from what it already is.

Thinking of a relationship as process frees us of our either/or, right/wrong approach to problems. This perspective helps us view everything that happens, good or bad, as vital and necessary to the evolution of a relationship.

You already know you have difficulties in your relationship. Some of you are in new relationships, some in old, and some are starting anew. Some of you are anticipating a fresh start and don't want to repeat history. You feel both fear and excitement. You have many tools to do relationships wrong, and not too many to do them right. In reality, though, what's "right" is not a set path. It's not a yellow brick road that leads easily to a destination. Right is viewing a relationship as a process, always unfolding, and therefore unique to each participant. The only destination you can count on is a positive outcome.

## CHARACTERISTICS OF THE PROCESS

Love as a living process cannot be reduced to a neat little conceptual package. Even so, the fluid and ongoing process is not random. It abides by the laws of transformation. In addition, there are key characteristics that describe the life of relationships. Since most people are doing their work while in relationships, understanding these characteristics can be critical to the survival of the relationships. We will consider each of these characteristics:

- Self-Love
- Healthy Boundaries
- Personal Responsibility

- Creating Better Endings
- Growing with Pain
- Resolving Conflict
- Trusting/Entrusting
- Committing to the Ongoing Process
- Power Sharing

## Self-Love

The process of love begins with you. Real love is unselfish yet it is "self-full." It does not seek or demand gratification. It just is.

Sometimes we find it hard to love ourselves, or we act as though we love ourselves more than we love others. We become narcissistic, centered in ourselves. To gain perspective, we can remember our three lovers: the addictive lover that seeks to repeat history, the healthy lover that seeks to evolve, and the spiritual lover that seeks enlightened relationships.

From your spiritual lover, become an observer. It is this lover who is compassionate, wise, and who has that cosmic sense of humor that can help your understanding of it all. It loves you beyond your human conditioning or your addictions. It recognizes you had to develop a false ego in order to survive. It knows, also, how difficult it is to give up the familiar and predictable. It is patient.

Self-love includes, but is not limited to, the following: loving our "being" no matter what we think, feel, or do; accepting our mistakes as lessons to be learned; nurturing the natural, innocent child within; being our own best friend; taking good care of our body; encouraging and affirming the best aspects of who we are; accepting our limitations; renewing the commitment to treat ourselves with value and respect each day; entrusting ourselves to others who will do the same; and speaking up when others fail to do so.

Self-love accepts you exactly where you are. You may not like where you are, but you can still love yourself the best you can from this place. You can only love others to the degree you love yourself; you can only take in love to the degree you love yourself. The common saying "love your neighbor as you love yourself" recognizes that relationships take place not on the outside first, but on the inside. Your love of a neighbor is only a mirror of how you love yourself. Lack of self-love actually produces jealousy. Abe came to me with little self-love as he talked about loving his wife, Nelly, more than himself.

*Abe's Story: "I'm really glad Nelly didn't come to my rescue."*

> I had intense feelings of jealousy as I saw Nelly giving to others at a weekend workshop. So I withdrew, something I had learned to do as a child. I began feeling sorry for myself, hoping Nelly would come and rescue me. She didn't come. So I had choices: being a martyr, getting angry and lashing out, telling her what I was experiencing, or talking to the little boy in me that I didn't know very well and telling him he is all right and I love him. I'm really glad Nelly didn't come to my rescue. It gave me a chance to spend some much needed time with myself and get to know the little guy inside of me. I could start giving him equal time and attention.

## Healthy Boundaries

The word *boundary* originally referred to a landmark, that which marked off one piece of territory from another. For our relationships, this definition suggests the importance of allowing our uniqueness to mark our territory from another's, to create our psychological space.

A boundary as a physical dividing line is easy to recognize, but on a psychological level it is much more complex. People talk about "having walls" to protect themselves and "putting up barriers." Others say they "feel invaded" or "don't know where I stop or another begins." We feel people "closing us out," or we feel people's "openness" that invites us in.

Osmosis, one of the essential processes of life, requires a semi-permeable membrane for a healthy exchange of ingredients necessary to life. Think of boundary as a semi-permeable sheath around you. Because it is semi-permeable, it can take in what it needs and let out what it does not want. It can breathe! What it does take in can become a part of what already exists; what it doesn't want it can discharge.

Boundaries should be semi-permeable, so our love, power, and intuition can be exchanged easily and by choice. There can be a clear line of demarcation, where each person has thoughts, feelings, values, and actions that are respected and shared. If boundaries are too permeable or mushy, we begin to define ourselves by others' thoughts, feelings, and actions. If our boundaries are too permeable, they will collapse; too much goes out, too much comes in. If our boundaries are impermeable, then we project an antidependent stance and refuse to reach out, take in, or give. We become hardened, making our spiritual lover unable to express itself or be shared.

In the process of a relationship, we can be mindful and respectful of boundaries and take full responsibility for them. If we erect a wall, we take responsibility for so doing, and we know why. If someone is penetrating our boundaries with thoughts, needs, feelings, and actions we do not want, we speak up and say "stop," or else acknowledge that we are cooperating.

*The key to healthy boundaries is knowing our needs and limits and speaking about them to others.* We know and define what is good for us. We take responsibility for our boundaries: "I hear what you are saying and my experience is different." "I know you believe that is good for me, but I need to make my own decision." "It's okay for me to feel good even when you're sad."

Diane reveals how she came to terms with healthy boundaries.

**Diane's Story:** *"I've chosen to be clear with my friend as to what I need."*

> I have come to a clearer sense of what my boundaries are and am better able to honor them. For me, having and honoring my boundaries means that I am able to sense and act on my feelings, needs, and wants in a respectful way rather than adapting to what I perceive to be someone else's. This is especially clear in terms of my relationships with men.
>
> Earlier in my life, I was involved with a man who told me, "True love is rare. Once you find it you have to hold on to it, or you may never have another chance." I also heard an unspoken message in these words: *Suppress your own feelings, needs, and wants. Learn to adapt to mine. If you don't and you decide to leave, you may never have another chance at love.* This was a powerful message for me to hear, and I accepted

it as being true. I took in his statement as my own reality. It formed the foundation for my acceptance of gross psychological and sexual abuse that lasted for over nine years.

I'm learning that I'm important, and that my feelings, wants, and needs are important too. I'm presently involved with someone who is very loving and respectful of me. He also has wants and needs that are different than mine in important ways. This is sometimes painful. But it's good to know that I am *feeling*, even if some of it is unpleasant. And rather than suppress my own wants and needs in an attempt to hold on to the relationship, I've chosen to be clear with my friend as to what I need. Who knows where the relationship will go? One thing is certain: I'm coming to accept and honor who I am. Having and keeping respectful boundaries is the manifestation of this process in my life.

## Personal Responsibility

Crucial to the process of love is taking responsibility for our circumstances. Recall the 100 percent intent ratio: We have in our life what we intend to have; what we don't have, we never intended. Our life has been a series of choices and continues to be.

Granted, as children our options were limited, or we were strongly influenced to choose or believe a certain way. Some of us are victims of major catastrophes: a hijacking, war, rape, incest. But even in situations where we are innocent victims, we have options as to how we will act. We can still choose our *response* to the event. We can also continue to feel, think, and act as a victim of situations. If so, we may continue to attract people and situations that victimize us. We remain reactors, letting life events define or condition us.

*Personal responsibility* is that willingness to claim our thoughts, feelings, and actions, good or bad. There is no blame. We recognize that on some level we choose our experiences, or when we don't we can learn from them. As we transcend the victim position, we are free to move forward.

Personal responsibility means we recognize that we bring a history, conditioning, illusions, and fears into any relationship. We have made messes in the past, and it is likely we may create those same messes from time to time. We bring our vulnerabilities with us, and we are likely to choose partners who fit our vulnerabilities. *Personal responsibility means cleaning up the messes we make.* We own them, and if they harm others or self, we make amends. Personal responsibility means we take responsibility for our share of the relationship and not more than our share. We recognize when others are unloading their vulnerabilities on us or are inviting us to clean up their messes.

Each of us received negative or limiting messages as part of our scripts. *Don't be close* is a common one. A person who accepted this message as a child is likely to find a partner who also has a fear of closeness and who is willing to push people away or withdraw. As the emotional distance continues, each person develops an addictive, unhealthy dependency on the other. The lack of intimacy is denied, defended, or considered the other person's fault: "You want too much from me." "You're too sensitive."

In love as process, the *don't be close* message may still be a major factor. As one partner emotionally withdraws and is committed to personal responsibility, the person states, "I've had as much closeness as I'm comfortable with for now." Or the other partner may say, "I'm experiencing your distance, and I need to know what's going on with you." Such acknowledgments expose the issue and make it a part of the relationship's conscious movement.

### Creating Better Endings

When we view relationships as living process, it doesn't matter if history repeats itself. We are different. We are aware; we are responsible. We have a spiritual lover. We have new tools or know where to get them. We have options, choices. We work toward different and more positive outcomes. When history presents itself again, we consider it a gift, an opportunity to get closure to a past event that wasn't resolved. Familiar with our history, we can be subjective and objective at the same time. We can participate and observe ourselves in our own scenarios.

*Every relationship is a teacher. If you don't learn the lesson, the teacher will return.* This thought can motivate us to learn from mistakes and resolve problems from the best aspects of ourselves. Beth shared what her relationship taught her.

*Beth's Story:* "*I wanted to do my part in creating a healthier outcome.*"

> I experienced intense emotional turmoil when I challenged the behavior of an important friend. Though I hadn't experienced such a feeling for a long time, it felt like an old, familiar friend. I recalled similar scenes in my past where this despair was present. In both instances I had been abandoned. How my addictive lover had dealt with these situations before would not be helpful now. I wanted to do my part in creating a healthier outcome. So I detached from the experience, became my spiritual lover, and wrote the following to myself: "Trust your instincts. What you are asking for is right. Stop pushing. Work to feel the inner peace and harmony you had. Let go of the pain in ways you can. He isn't ready to give you what you ask for. He has much grief that he needs to feel first. Stop withholding your love. Forgive and love his humanness as difficult as that may be. Stop personalizing his behavior. It is his, not who he is."

You bring your addictive lover and hurt self as well as your healthy and spiritual lovers into relationships. The learned self often wants to prove that its history and negative beliefs are the truth. Commitment to relationships as a living process assures that when history appears to be repeating itself, you will stick around to produce better endings.

### Growing with Pain

A significant aspect of relationships as living process is using pain to grow. Our addictive lover may avoid pain, inflict pain, attempt to control with pain, or refuse to talk about pain. In experiencing love as a process, we fully acknowledge pain as an indicator that something may not be right here. We may first check to see if the feeling is exaggerated or if, indeed, there is legitimate "discounting" going on.

In relationships, *discount* means that some aspect of who I am, what I feel, what I need, what I think, or what I do is being denied, minimized, or considered unresolvable. Anytime we recognize a discount and we do not challenge it, we cooperate with the abuse. Recognizing and confronting discounts may be the most important lesson we can learn.[1]

We identify discounts through emotional pain. Pain may be as mild a discomfort as confusion, or it may run deep. Both generate the question: What is going on here? The pain is never personalized, only felt. It is used to identify the discount and to confront it. We can then work to get closure rather than deny or keep an open wound. This acknowledges that we deserve to be treated well.

When someone treats me disrespectfully and I say, "Something must be wrong with me" or "I should have done it better," I have personalized and now doubled the discount. If instead I say, "That behavior doesn't feel very good, I'd like it to stop," I am being accountable to myself and at the same time confronting the discount.

Pain is nature's way to tell us we are getting too much or too little of something. We can respect our inner child's ability to identify needs through pain. As we commit to nonabusive behavior, we find that feeling pain quickly is a way to give ourselves valuable information and affirm our boundaries. We might not know immediately what is going on, but we can, with time, figure it out.

Looking for patterns in the way we're discounted is especially useful. Though you may be quick to feel pain in what is happening, you may choose to not take action initially and accept that others do make mistakes. If the discount continues, however, it's time to confront this fact.

Once you identify the discount and talk about how it impacts you and the relationship, it is important to identify the need. It may take time—hours, a day, a week—to figure that out. When you do, you can speak directly and respectfully for what you need.

Our addictive lover is paranoid about pain. It anticipates hurts, disappointments, and problems. Our healthy lover is committed to being aware that pain and problems exist and to taking care of ourselves in their presence. Our spiritual lover transcends pain. Dan had trouble trusting people. He came from a history of physical beatings and abandonment. He had made a decision to "never reach out because you'll only get hurt."

***Dan's Story:*** *"It was hell opening up."*

> As an adult, I started working to regain the trust I'd lost. I'd been in a support group a month before I opened up. When I did, I acknowledged how scared I was of revealing my feelings, and then I risked sharing a painful life transition I was going through. At the end of a group session, another group member said she was angry at me for not working harder. I felt hurt and was angry. I saw my urge to feel shame and heard an inner voice say: *What a fool you are. You know you can't trust people and this proves it. You reach out and get kicked even in a group where you thought there was support.* I processed all these feelings and recognized that among them, hurt was the most legitimate one. I'd indeed been discounted. To the other member I said, "I know you care about me, and what you just said doesn't feel very affirming. It was hell opening up tonight. I need where I am to be acceptable and what I did do affirmed."

There are three categories of feelings, and Dan's story is an excellent example of all three. Hurt was the *real feeling* for the situation. Anger was a *rubberband feeling*, one that is out of proportion because it's connected to some feeling-laden event in the past, in this case unexpressed anger at his father.[2] The shame was a *racket feeling*, a manipulative feeling created to justify old history. When we confront discounts, we need to deal with the *real feeling*.

Joanne described her process of experiencing love as "the joy of feeling."

***Joanne's Story:*** *"Feelings tell us who we are."*

> For me at one time, I could imagine no joy to be found in feeling. Feeling seemed to be mainly a state of feeling the *pain* of life, with a few sprinklings of excitement or brief moments of pleasure thrown in to tantalize.

164

Like many, many others, I grew up in an alcoholic family. Sexually abused and deserted by my alcoholic father at a very young age, I then became the pawn between a codependent mother and a tyrannical stepfather. He was determined to battle a never-ending war of blaming, accusation, hostility, and bitter disappointment. It was an unhappy household, and I was frequently scared and angry.

Physical force and emotional threats were used to teach me that the only way I could be accepted was to show a compliant, pleasing, and "nice" exterior. Being a smart little girl, I learned how to do this very well. As time went on, I discovered an interesting shortcut to maintaining the facade I needed to get by. What I discovered was that if I never even felt my feelings, then it required less effort to try to hide them from the adults around me.

With a sense of purpose, I worked diligently to turn myself into a stone. And it worked—part of me did become a stone, frozen and immovable, with no compassion for myself or others. I felt proud of my ability to control the exterior I presented to the world, and believed I'd discovered the key to survival.

I escaped my feelings through a wide range of addictions, including food, drugs, spending, sexual relationships, work, even reading. Anything can be an addiction if used regularly and compulsively to avoid feelings. At one time, I was even addicted to the seemingly healthy practice of yoga—spending up to three hours a day in a solitary practice—at the same time my eating disorder, drugs, and alcohol abuse were dangerously threatening my health.

Finally, however, the sea wall of anger, despair, and self-destructiveness that emerged when I was under the influence of alcohol was so frightening that I had no choice but to enter treatment in order to live.

What I know now that I didn't know then is that feelings cannot be "disappeared" from our lives simply because we don't like that they're there. Feelings tell us who we are—

what we like and don't like, what feels good and what (or who) doesn't, which direction points to fulfillment and which direction leads to pain. Stuffing them into cramped, tight, dusty corners doesn't kill them; it only causes them to act like prisoners, who tunnel and dig to escape when the corridors of expression are locked and barred. And if the feelings are unexpressed, the problem at hand will never be resolved.

In summary, doing your part means acknowledging discounts via your feelings, asking for what you need, letting go, and trusting the process. A partner committed to the process will hear you, and the pain will eventually lead to growth. If for some reason the hurtful behaviors continue, consider seeking outside support.

**Resolving Conflict**

> *Problems do not go away. They must be worked through or else they remain forever a barrier to the growth and development of the spirit.*
> — *M. Scott Peck*

Do you face conflict in the process of love? Of course! Whereas the spiritual lover stresses the importance of full acceptance of self and others, it never assumes that all behaviors, thoughts, and ways of expressing feelings are good or to our liking. It knows that just as our goodness needs to be affirmed, negatives need to be confronted. It knows that we have a deeper spiritual sense of worth. The addictive lover uses confrontation to inflict hurt, to get our way, to control outcomes, or it is avoided altogether. The healthy lover uses confrontation to stop hurt, even when fear is present.

The healthy lover confronts itself and others whenever thoughts, behaviors, or feelings are inconsistent with mutual respect, personal responsibility, honesty, and growth. It confronts all forms of abuse in a potent, caring way. In response to all this, the spiritual lover simply observes the lessons being learned.

In love as a living process, partners are committed to remaining open rather than defending, staying rather than leaving, and owning rather than blaming. Arguing, battling, abusing are replaced with talking, listening, respecting. *The process, or how we do it, is more important than the content, outcome, or results.*

*Conflict* means a struggle to overcome discord. It means to be in mutual opposition. *Resolve* means to change from dissonance to harmony. The dissonance at the onset of the conflict is offset by the harmony and growth that follow. *With a spiritual lover's commitment to honesty, you are likely to experience more conflicts.* You can look forward to conflict, as your history affirms conflict is an important way to know yourself and others. The big bonus is growing in love.

It doesn't necessarily start out this way. The first steps of the dance of conflict are quite familiar. Under threat of attack, our survival instinct will tell us to fight, flee, or freeze. Yet, we sometimes need to go through these immature dance steps before we come together and resolve our differences in a loving way. The "fight, flee, or freeze" helps us get the emotional charge out so the spiritual lover can step in.

The question is, how do you step back from the conflict and get centered again? Here is one couple's answer.

**David and Lisa's Story:** *"That statement . . . provided the safety to let my pain out."*

> DAVID: I know it's a whole lot easier backing up when you have a partner who owns what he or she is feeling and doing without blaming. For me to be able to say in the middle of it, "Wait a minute," and say what I'm feeling is important. That way, my partner doesn't keep on charging. The commitment is there. Sometimes, I find myself up to my ass in alligators when my original objective was to drain the swamp. I'm ankle deep, head first at times. I need to take time to stop and talk about what I'm feeling.
>
> Part of it is being willing to stop when I'm in the middle of my nonsense. I've invested a lot of psychological energy into my emotional payoff, kind of like having poker chips

on the table. I have to be willing to say to myself, "Wait a minute, that was a crooked investment—I'm not going to collect it." It's real hard to do when I've been schooled to just go away and be alone, and I've worked hard to justify doing just that. It's been real important for me to say to myself and my partner, "I'm not leaving; I just have some things to work out."

LISA: For me, it is the awareness that the other way doesn't work. I've lived it, and even in the heat of the drama, I don't want the negative payoff. I'm willing to do it another way even if it's hard. I might do my fight, flight, and freeze routine first. I recognize it now and use it as a way to regroup. I know I'll come back. I may need to walk, do some writing first. Often, in those times I need to remind myself that it really was okay to take a risk, even if he didn't like hearing what I had to say. I sometimes struggle and wonder if I should go make it right and remind myself that I must stay honest no matter what and trust in positive outcomes. There have been times when I really wondered if we could get through this one. Having a partner who's willing to stay and work things out is real new. I remember a time when I became childlike and angry. I told him to go away. He said, "No, I'm not leaving because I have a commitment to stay." That statement challenged me to give up my grandiose belief that I had the power to make people go away and provided the safety to let my pain out.

An interviewer once asked me, "Isn't healthy love boring?" Absolutely not. Because individuals are committed to honesty, first to themselves and then others, the process invites more action, excitement, intimacy, and opportunities to explore new territories than ever before. And there is always the element of not knowing the outcome, especially when we are attempting to resolve conflicts.

### Trusting/Entrusting

Healthy love is based on trust. Not perfection—trust. This means trust in self, trust that the other person is there for us, and trust in the process. Trust is self-creating. Trust is being totally vulnerable. Trust is accepting the existence of universal laws that we can count on. We trust that all we dream of is there.

Trust was once easy, a natural state of being. For some of us, that's not true anymore. Our life experiences made certain of that.

*The biggest challenge we have in a relationship as a living process is to trust and entrust.* To our human self, this is the greatest of challenges, the most difficult deconditioning process we face: to get open again and then to remain open to our spiritual lover in the midst of, or with the potential of, pain and rejection. If we do, we will affirm Kahlil Gibran's reminder that "sorrow carves the heart to contain more joy."

Trusting another is far easier when we grow up and trust that we can take good care of ourselves in relationships. We can know that the only thing that stops someone from loving us is his or her own limitations on love and not that we are unlovable.

A trusting relationship can become living therapy when a partner agrees to allow the injured child inside the other to reach out and ask for what it needed but did not receive in childhood.

A couple who came to a weekend workshop were painfully distant from each other and considering a permanent separation. At one point in the workshop, I asked the participants to introduce their inner child to their partner and to ask their partner to care for it for a certain period of time. The partners were to act as substitute parents. Later, they came back and discussed the experience. The couple who had been distant felt intense love for the inner child of the other and discovered how loving the partner's parenting was. As innocence and love connected and trust was reestablished, the couple felt hope and joy that had been long forgotten.

In a relationship as a process, our three lovers are present, understood, and shared in an atmosphere of trust. Parenting each other in clear, contractual ways helps identify what we need. Saying when we have had enough is healing to our inner child. When the inner child's experience is validated and affirmed, our trust of self and others grows, and the spiritual lover becomes more obvious. How much healthier this is than compulsively seeking others to get unmet needs fulfilled.

## Committing to the Ongoing Process

> *Commitment is the foundation, the bedrock of any genuinely loving relationship.*
>
> — *M. Scott Peck*

For the spiritual lover, it is easy to trust our connectedness and sense of belonging, for we are all one. Our human lover, experiencing the complexities we bring into a relationship, needs more reassurance. In relationships, a commitment to the process of being with a person provides the safety that allows staying connected as the complexities surface.

At the base of many relationship problems is having suffered a betrayal in earlier commitments. The injuries of the betrayal can be healed with a new experience of commitment. The commitment is not made to a person, nor focused on outcomes, and makes no guarantees. Instead, commitment is to the transformation of ourselves and those we love. Each person says, "I am committed to the process of being with you and becoming the best me I can be. I will share this me with you in ways that value and honor us both. I will do my part fully to continue growing, evolving, getting to know and live my inner truth; to take responsibility for my history, my vulnerabilities; to speak on my own behalf; to own my love, my power, my spiritual lover; and to share it even in the presence of fear. I commit to doing my part to maintain the connection even as the form of our relationship changes. I commit to loving me, loving you."

A relationship will grow in love as each person is committed to their ongoing transformation and to the relationship. In traditional wedding vows, we often commit to what seems like a fixed institution, and because of that we often fear or abuse commitment. Seldom do we take responsibility for the personal growth that sustains loving relationships. In spiritual love, one is committed to the process of *being with* another person, not *to* the person.

In the Catholic tradition a marriage is considered a sacrament. I know a Catholic couple named Marie and Lou. Marie told me, "We just discovered our marriage is supposed to be a different kind of sacrament than we had thought. We thought sacrament meant a block of time, a neat little box you could put on a shelf and count on. It affirmed you as married and guaranteed happiness and love ever-lasting. Not so!" What they are learning is that sacrament doesn't guarantee spiritual lovers. It only affirms spiritual love's possibility. *Sacrament* of marriage must become an action word, where each lover is viewed as an honorary participant in the accepting and giving of love, where every moment is viewed as an opportunity to become a sacred moment when partners create unconditional love. Then, they are gracing the moment with God. A state of grace becomes that feeling of oneness.

The paradox is that while focusing on the changing process of love, we are more likely to be there for another. Each person takes responsibility for the personal history she or he brings and sometimes re-creates good and bad.

To illustrate further, Marie and Lou had been married for ten years and needed to renew their commitment to each other.

**Marie and Lou's Story:** *"Their learned selves were repeating history by withdrawing from intimacy."*

For many years, Marie had wanted to go back to graduate school to prepare for a professional career. As they began talking about their concerns over loans and their changing relationship, they experienced all three selves: the learned self that was scared because of the changes taking place; the autonomous self that allowed for such changes in a sup-portive way; and the spiritual self that sought creative expression.

It became clear, when Marie talked to Lou, that the prob-lem was in the fearful child: "As the oldest child of ten," she said, "I had to be in charge and felt alone. My dad needed me to help, but never encouraged or supported my suc-cesses. This part of me has been afraid you'd withdraw, Lou, as I began pursuing my dream, and when you actually did withdraw, I felt even more scared and lonely. I decided I wouldn't need anything from you. I'd take care of myself, like I did when I was a kid." At this point, Marie began seeing the humor in the repeated childlike behavior.

"Although I hate to admit it," Lou responded, "I'm afraid of abandonment too. I was sixteen when my mom killed herself. I thought I had worked this out and I guess I haven't. Even when you go away for a week or two, I get scared. So I withdraw because I think I can't be hurt as much that way."

Both of their learned selves, anticipating hurt and betrayal, repeated history by withdrawing from intimacy.

They renewed their commitment to the process of being with each other and stated clearly that should they withdraw, it would only be temporary. They would openly discuss any fear or pain. It was refreshing to watch their demeanors change as both felt a sense of renewed trust in themselves and in each other.

Marie and Lou made a promise that if the contracts were violated, they would bring it into the open. Their story emphasizes that the process of a relationship is more important than the content. As they trusted and entrusted, a positive outcome occurred naturally. They began gracing more moments with their spiritual lovers.

## Power Sharing

Viewing love as a process, we recognize that we are not islands, but are profoundly connected to each other. We are called to assist each other in this work of personal transformation. As we release our spiritual lover, we discover a deeper meaning of love and power. We no longer need to be in control. Instead, we take charge by doing our part and sharing both love and power with others and the world at large. As such, we are both student and teacher. Power sharing rather than power playing becomes a way of life; we learn to power share rather than indulge in power plays. This characteristic is so important that it forms the subject of our next chapter.

## CHALLENGES OF LOVE

By now we may realize how difficult a love relationship is. There are three dependencies we can move in and out of: primary dependency, addictive dependency, and interdependency. There are three lovers inside us: the addictive, autonomous, and spiritual lovers. Add to this individual uniqueness, and we can begin to understand why a relationship is not a neat little package.

When you truly accept the complexity of a love relationship, it will no longer be difficult. You will see it for what it is and no longer attempt to make it something it is not. Many want a fixed relationship, something they can count on. The one thing you can count on, however, is change and, if you stay with it, growth.

If you want safe and predictable outcomes, the process of healthy love may not be for you.

We have the urge to grow and the urge to keep things the way they are, and we must choose. Choosing to grow takes great effort and determination. Fears will surface. As the relationship begins to change, we are challenged to remain loving and to stay connected even when outcomes are uncertain.

To sum up the idea of love as a lawful process, let me say that my relationships are not perfect. There are messes at times. Having made the promise to do my part in bringing as much light as possible into my relationships, I trust in positive outcomes because the laws of the universe are there to meet me. I have learned that as I do my part and let go, there are indeed riches beyond imagination. My life is filled with relationships that are rich with intimacy, honesty, challenge, excitement, confrontation, newness, vitality.

## ACTIVITIES

### 1. Reminders for Sustaining Healthy Love

We have learned that a love relationship is not a neat little package. It is a process that challenges us daily. Here are twelve ideas that can be helpful to us in sustaining healthy love relationships. Feel free to photocopy them and post them as daily reminders.

1. Commit to the process of becoming a loving partner and being with another.
2. Focus on the process of a relationship and not the content, form, or outcomes.
3. Acknowledge the three lovers you bring into each relationship: the addictive lover that seeks to repeat history, the healthy lover that seeks its autonomy, and the spiritual lover that seeks enlightened relationships.
4. Learn to distinguish the three dependency systems that are simultaneously present in your relationships: addictive, primary, and interdependent.
5. Identify the personal history of fears, injuries, and sensitivities you bring into each relationship.
6. Take responsibility for any negative thoughts, feelings, and behaviors you bring into relationships.
7. Make clear contracts on staying with your partner, and confronting and resolving conflict.
8. Confront broken contracts/commitments and renegotiate them.
9. Entrust your vulnerabilities to others who are in the process of healthy love with you.
10. Make amends to self and others as need be.
11. Clean up any messes you bring into relationships and work to get closure on them.
12. Trust in positive outcomes.

### 2. *Resolving Conflict*

The more life is studied, the more apparent it has become that all of nature's organisms associate, link, live cooperatively, and share essential characteristics. In this balanced state there is a combination of competition as mutual dependence. This competition, however, takes place within a wider context of cooperation. It is only when excessive aggression, competition, and destructive behavior (including giving up and giving in) predominate that relationships fail. This is not common in the autonomous self, which suggests the negative behavior is *learned* rather than natural.

Resolving conflict in a healthy way means resolving inner conflict first—separating what we have learned from our natural state. Recall that we have three lovers inside us. When things are working together, we experience love merged with power, and we resolve external conflicts with ease and clarity. When these aspects of us are out of synch, we feel torn, pulled in different directions, anxious, confused. We are more likely to injure ourselves or others.

Use this exercise to help you resolve conflicts, both internal and external, in order to pull yourself out of the morass of relationship problems.

1.  Identify a relationship problem creating inner turmoil for you now.
2.  Separate your addictive lover, healthy lover, and spiritual lover. You can do this through writing, imaging, or doing a three-chair technique. Each chair symbolizes one of your lovers. Switch chairs as you become each lover and speak from that perspective.
    a.  Ask each lover to state its position—how it views the problem; what it needs to resolve the conflict in a cooperative manner.
    b.  Talk with each lover until all three are working together. Remember, the addictive lover was designed by you to keep your life predictable and safe. It is loyal to its heritage. You will get further by thanking it for what it has done, educating it, and finding a place for it in your life.
3.  Let your spiritual lover be the spokesperson as you talk with the person you are in conflict with.

## CHAPTER EIGHT

# Power Sharing

*When we turn from victim into master, what do we do with our power?*

— *Richard Bach*

## HOW WE DEVELOP PERSONAL POWER

In Chapter One we discussed the true meaning of power. We learned that power is not a commodity outside of ourselves; it is our life force. On a human level, power is our own personal potency, an energy that originates from within and reaches outward in an attempt to get our basic needs met. Power is the ability to produce change. In spiritual terms, power is the core truth that flows through us as we allow ourselves to be channels of higher wisdom. It is what defines us as warriors who are unafraid to face our fears. Being alive is an expression of our power.

There is a Finnish word, *sisu*, that refers to active power. I am told that it has no English equivalent. As a child, I was told I had *sisu*. I didn't know the language but the word felt good. Having active power means we have courage, tenacity, determination, verve, believability, dedication, commitment.

Power sharing assumes a healthy sense of personal power. Developing personal power begins in infancy. Had we received everything we needed in the way we needed it, our childhood experience might look like this:

- *In the womb and in the first six months of our life,* our only responsibility is to be or to exist. The world revolves around us. Just being alive, we get the world's attention. We feel wonderful, secure, and important—no thinking, no doing, just being and expressing who we are. Experience shows us: I am omnipotent.

- *At six months of age,* we take our omnipotence and combine it with our senses as we explore the world. The world only has to provide us with safety. We have the right to initiate when and what to explore, to fully see, feel, hear, touch, smell, move, taste, and to decide when we have enough. We are never told no or punished for exploring. We use our power to please our senses and trust our reaching out.

- *When we turn two,* we begin having a memory and advance in our language skills. We can think, create, and act on thoughts. With this advancement comes good and bad news. The bad news is that we are told in a variety of ways that it is time to grow up and share our omnipotence with all the other omnipotent people. Contrary to what we believe, we are not the center of the universe. Although we are important, we are no more or less important than others. We have to learn to share our power with others, to wait, to mind our manners, to live cooperatively. The good news is that as we share, we notice life moves more easily, our importance doesn't diminish, and we have more, not less, freedom and power.

- *At age four,* we begin to notice we are a particular sex, male or female. Living in a world of shared power, we notice that men and women are both powerful and tender. They treat each other with mutual respect and easily model power sharing inside and outside the home, and in all love relationships.

- *By age six,* we learn that we have power in being who we are, that the world provides the safety and permission to explore the use of our power and that growing up and sharing power with others is a joy. Men and women have equal personal power. Having this as our experience, we then move out into the world to easily share power with others.

## MYTHS OF POWER

What should have been reality sounds more like myth! It would be humorous if it weren't so tragic. Few people experienced what they needed to power share easily. Omnipotence may never have been fully experienced. Parents were cautioned not to treat the child in the ways described in the previous section for fear the child would "get a big head." As a baby, we may have often been left alone and learned reaching out was ineffective. As we explored, unnecessary limits were set. We were told what to explore or what not to touch. We learned to overpower or be overpowered. We watched men and women, our role models, struggle with power and love.

By about age six, we lost contact with our identity and had a list of myths about power that began directing us to play games with power. Jim's story illustrates this.

*Jim's Story:* *"Power sharing sure is a lot less work."*

> Growing up, I felt I had a choice of two alternatives, control or be controlled. I didn't like being controlled, so I chose to control. My mother tried to control everything. By dominating and controlling, she eliminated individualism, imagination, and uniqueness. "Do this." "Don't do that." "Don't cry." "Don't be a baby."
>
> The control or power signals were not always verbal: rolling of the eyes, shaking the head no, hands on hips, or an air of disgust.
>
> For me to get recognition, I felt I had to perform and play the role. If it wasn't done her way, you paid the price of being in her "doghouse." In many ways I felt like a puppet, and she pulled and controlled the strings at will.
>
> Then I got married and started a family. I used what I learned. Power was getting people to do what I wanted. I thought power plays would keep me from being controlled, keep me from being hurt, provide certainty, freedom. It only distanced me from my wife, my children, and most important, myself. A power play that almost got physical got my attention. I committed to change.

The most noticeable change through my process has been awareness of how little I felt. I'm amazed at how little I knew or paid attention to. I was shut down, cut off.

There are many alternatives and choices and not just a choice between control or being controlled. Sharing is unusual for me. I'm not used to it, but it feels good. Power sharing brought me more time for getting to know the little boy inside of me, more joy, more closeness, more respect.

I will continue to grow and work with learning other alternatives and new concepts and ideas.

One important lesson I learned that was not acceptable in the past is *it's okay to be angry and still show it and love at the same time.* In the past it was anger or love by itself. It couldn't be both; it was one or the other. By changing, I was able to openly and freely accept and love my grandson and daughter, a single parent. This would not have been tolerated under the old system. Sometimes I'm scared and awkward, but in the final analysis, power sharing sure is a lot less work.

Like Jim, we all harbor unconscious beliefs about power. Here are some common myths about power. Perhaps you can identify with one or more of them.

- Power is silence and withdrawal.
- Power is scary.
- Power is shouting and silence.
- Power is what men have in a relationship.
- Power can be shown by men but not women.
- Men are supposed to be powerful, but it's really women who have it.
- Women use manipulation to be in power.
- Power can be used against me, so I must undermine it or become indifferent to it.
- Power is used to control.
- Power means breaking the rules because that's the way to fight the person making them.

- Power is money.
- Men have all the power, and the only way a woman can get it is through sex.
- Men have power through being big and loud. Women have power by being sweet and coy.
- If you are powerful, people will leave you.
- Men have power by staying uninvolved. Women have power by being afraid.
- Men use brute force; women use taunts, tears, and anger to express power.

## Understanding and Stopping Power Plays

It is probably clear by now why the road to the spiritual lover is not an easy one, why it requires us to be heroines and warriors, why we spend so much time as addictive lovers. None of us could possibly get all that we needed in our human development. Besides our history and our learned roles, our early experiences with love and power confused us. We could more easily power play than power share.

In doing so, we create the tragicomedies so obvious in our news, our TV dramas, our daily interactions: "Billionaire casts wife aside for new lover." "Will Jonathan live to tell Carolyn he loves her? Tune in tomorrow." Our drama translates into psychological insults where we are all players and losers, where we both receive and inflict injury of the heart and spirit. "I can't stand you another minute, so I'm leaving." "I can't grow with you in my way."

Unfortunately, most transactions in our love relationships are invitations into power plays. As one person described it, "Power plays are the dance people do with each other when they don't know they are dancing. This is followed by the ugly feeling they have when they're all done dancing." Another person said, "Power plays are what happens when you try to get what you want, but you don't know how to ask or are afraid to ask." Still another said, "It's how I protect myself, how I get what I want, what I do when I'm bored. It's empty talk that gets nowhere."

Power plays deserve our attention. For if we are ever to love in healthy ways, if we are ever to let out our spiritual lover, we must understand and then stop the abuse of power.

### STEPPING ON THE DRAMA TRIANGLE

The Drama Triangle, as designed by Dr. Stephen Karpman, is one of the clearest ways to understand the roles in our power dramas.[1]

# Drama Triangle*

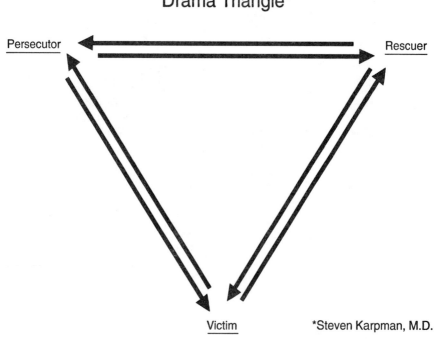

Persecutor

Rescuer

Victim

*Steven Karpman, M.D.

The Drama Triangle suggests that all roles in the drama can be understood in three terms: *persecutor, rescuer, victim*. Many of us will recognize those positions. We can see this in the following example.

WIFE: "You've got to take the dogs to obedience school!" (*Persecutor* looking for a *rescuer*.)

HUSBAND: "I don't want the dog, I never did, and now you're asking me to train it!" (*Persecutor* looking for a *victim*.)

WIFE: "This dog just won't mind me. I really need you to work with him. You have such a nice deep voice I don't have. He just won't respond to me. I don't sound powerful enough." (*Victim* looking for a *rescuer*.)

HUSBAND (*angrily*): "No, just leave me alone, I've got things to do. You wanted the darn dog." (*Persecutor* looking for a *victim*.)

WIFE: "Well, you're the one who is always complaining about the dog. You're the one who wants him to be well-behaved. If it wasn't for you, the dog would be fine without obedience school. I've got a house and kids to care for." (*Persecutor* looking for a *victim*.)

HUSBAND (*feeling guilty*): "Well, I suppose it wouldn't hurt me." (*Victim* turned *rescuer*.)

This scenario demonstrates how the roles start out complementary, with both parties in agreement. Then comes the dramatic switch to power plays. The drama goes on and on. One thing is certain: No matter what role you play most often, at some point you will feel victimized.

We did not start life as game players. We started as innocent. We did our part fully. We identified a need, communicated directly to a parent figure, and asked for what was needed. We either got no response, an inadequate response, or a negative response. It was in our reaching out without success that we experienced a loss of innocence.

As children, we needed someone to respond. As children, we were incapable of taking care of ourselves. We needed nurturing, protection. We needed wise, informed parents to hear and take care of us.

Take an example: Three-year-old Jimmy comes into the house saying he fell and hurt his knee and needs attention. Mother, on the telephone, irritably says, "Don't bother me right now. Can't you see

I'm busy?" She persecutes. Or she might overreact and seduce with words: "Oh honey, let Mommie kiss your sore and make it all better." Here she is a rescuer. Sometimes, upset or depressed, she fails to respond to Jimmy at all and he becomes the *victim*. Jimmy quickly learns to hit his mother and become a *persecutor*; cry excessively at the strokes of his mother and learn to be a *victim*; or stop having needs in order to take care of her depression—a *rescuer*.

## WHAT OUR DRAMA TELLS US

After studying and observing power plays, I've come to the following conclusions:

- Power plays are really a misguided attempt to establish healthy love.
- Healthy love is to provide nourishment, safety, and knowledge that assures growth.
- We would have no need to persecute or rescue unless we had been victimized as children.
- We are only victimized by someone who has also been victimized.
- Messes in our love relationships result from not getting something we needed as children.
- We are invited into power plays when violated or shamed, rejected because of our sex, laughed at for making a mistake, made a brunt of somebody else's jokes.
- Power plays suggest we believe in inequality of power.
- Each role we play suggests we have an unmet need. As a *victim*, we have not been loved unconditionally. As a *rescuer*, our experience of giving and receiving love was incomplete. As a *persecutor*, we are likely looking for safety and protection so we can trust again.
- To get to power sharing, we must agree to be absolutely vulnerable again and to risk. No easy task!

To sum up: As infants we do our part right. We freely use our life energy, our personal power, to ask others to respond to our legitimate need for nurturing, protection, and information. If those who care for us are knowledgeable, available, wise, and responsive, the need is met and we feel satisfied. We feel safe, loved. Our personal power is affirmed. Expressing ourselves makes a difference. If the need is not met, we become a victim for the first time. In our victimization, we begin doubting our right to be loved, our right to express our power. We give up or begin demanding.

Then, feeling incomplete, out of balance, and longing for wholeness, we call on our creative genius and design manipulative ploys that ask others to care for us. Looking at our models, we discover power plays and, too frightened, too injured, or too unaware, we bring them into our adult life and view them as normal.

We can see how all this works in adult life by turning to the following story.

*Mary's Story:* *"The light found its way to me."*

> I have been alcohol-free seven years and nicotine-free three months. I am a new person emerging who needs help in emotionally putting myself back together and claiming personal power.
>
> The core of me that was walled in by my various addictions has watched as the light found its way to me. And what seems very slow to me is a process of changing myself with compassion and patience and support from others. Some of that process has been to own my part in unhealthy relationships. That has been particularly painful for me, as I've needed to face the martyr-victim role I played to control most of them.
>
> I find myself thinking I've felt this way most of my life. As far back as I can remember, I've felt that seesaw of "be who I want you to be" from parents and friends. I can also remember the conflict within me to please or resist.
>
> It's astonishing for me to realize that another option is to claim my power and disagree and be me. Most of the time in my life, power sharing is done by me on what I consider

an "outer circle." In work and social situations, and with people I don't know very well, I feel more at ease being direct and assertive. The closer people are in my life, the greater the risk to really be me. It feels okay to share happiness, joy, positive stuff. But the other feelings not associated with "up" but with "down" are so hard to share, to express, to risk. It's hard to directly say, "I feel angry about this, I feel sad about this, I feel disappointed about this." And so, in a victim's stance, I manipulate.

I struggle to own the reality that often it is I who hesitates, who holds back, who withholds my affection and compassion. It is I who is not only a martyr-victim, but also a persecutor and at times a rescuer.

I believe power sharing occurs between people who experience themselves and each other as equal in value, who see the world filled with value and promise, who are actively involved in living life the best they are able. It occurs between people who find life as it is and accept it whole, and can still laugh and cry and feel.

## THE POWER SHARING TRIANGLE

Something inside stirs and calls us. Deeply buried under these ploys is someone who wants more love. The spiritual lover seeks the help of our learned self to get beyond the drama of power plays to realness and intimacy. We are called to another level of loving where power is shared. No more one-up, one-down melodrama; instead, the spiritual lover calls us to emotional and spiritual equality.

Try as we might, without healthy structure our learned self often resorts to the old and familiar ways of relating that do more harm than good. And though the spiritual lover does not need models, our learned self does.

In my own work with clients, I developed the following theory to explain an alternative to power plays: the Power Sharing Triangle.[2]

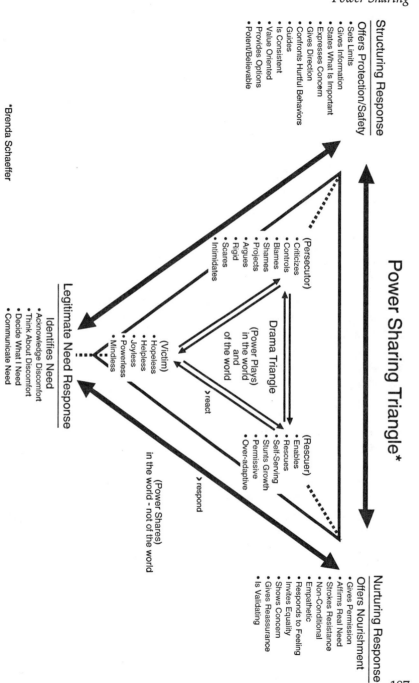

*Power Sharing*

**Power Sharing Triangle***

**Structuring Response**
Offers Protection/Safety
- Sets Limits
- Gives Information
- States What Is Important
- Expresses Concern
- Gives Direction
- Confronts Hurtful Behaviors
- Guides
- Is Consistent
- Value Oriented
- Provides Options
- Potent/Believable

**Nurturing Response**
Offers Nourishment
- Gives Permission
- Affirms Real Need
- Strokes Resistance
- Non-Conditional
- Empathetic
- Responds to Feeling
- Invites Equality
- Shows Concern
- Gives Reassurance
- Is Validating

**Legitimate Need Response**
Identifies Need
- Acknowledge Discomfort
- Think About Discomfort
- Decide What I Need
- Communicate Need

(Drama Triangle)
Drama Triangle
(Power Plays)
in the world
and
of the world

(Persecutor)
- Criticizes
- Controls
- Blames
- Shames
- Projects
- Argues
- Rigid
- Scares
- Intimidates

(Victim)
- Mindless
- Powerless
- Joyless
- Helpless
- Hopeless

(Rescuer)
- Enables
- Rescues
- Self-Serving
- Stunts Growth
- Permissive
- Over-adaptive

> react

> respond

(Power Shares)
in the world - not of the world

*Brenda Schaeffer

187

This alternative to power plays provides an opening to the spiritual lover. A person is not judged for inviting us into power plays, nor do we personalize his or her behavior. What is, is. This approach invites us to power share by stepping out of our predictable roles and choosing a different one. Everyone is intended to win. The Power Sharing Triangle has three response positions that invite us into healthy love:

- *Legitimate Need Response*
- *Nurturing Response*
- *StructuringResponse*

Our power sharing responses invite another person out of power plays. We speak in a familiar yet different language. We pace with the person's view of the world and respond to her or his unconscious needs for predictability. Healthy belonging is the offer. Needs are okay. Talk is straight. Hurtful behaviors are confronted with sensitivity and potency. Equality is affirmed. Trust is established. Openness, mutual acceptance, reliability, and congruence provide grounding to the inner child. Power sharing guides us to our inner wisdom. As we feel safe, we are encouraged to explore and risk in love again. As this happens the inner spark, the spiritual lover, begins to manifest more often.

## Legitimate Need Response

We first got into power plays due to a failure to get something we needed. Now, we can *identify* and express our *needs* simply and directly. We put it out for the world to see. We *feel our discomfort*, we *determine the need, voice the need,* and *let go of any expected outcome.*

The healthy lover knows we have four options:

1. Reach out to the person who can help us meet our need and get relief.
2. If that person is not available, we can reach out to another resource person, who can respond to the need.
3. Go within and parent ourselves.

4. Accept that we cannot for now get our need met and grieve our loss with dignity.

There are times when we don't have the energy to give to ourselves and nobody is around to give to us. We are then challenged to find ways to get reenergized. As we choose one of these four options, we return to a state of balance and harmony that is biological, psychological, and spiritual. Though we may be disappointed when a need is not met, our self-worth remains. Unlike the tension and limbo state we experienced as children, we now know we can wait or creatively seek solutions.

### Nurturing Response

Let's face it: Our insecurities and problems come from violations of trust and emotional abandonment. Therefore, attempting to stay involved versus leaving our partner can be essential and healing. Rather than rescue, however, we offer a healthy *Nurturing Response*. This might include *giving permission* to have and act on needs; *affirming the need* when it is put out there; *responding empathetically* to the way our partner views life; *caring* with detachment; expressing genuine *concern*; *inviting equality* of feeling, thinking, and doing; supporting risk taking; *validating* everyone's right to be treated respectfully without the customary caretaking, enabling, growth-stunting behaviors.

### Structuring Response

Rather than criticizing, blaming, shaming, controlling, and intimidating our partner, we can offer guidance, *protection*, and *safety*. Rather than the predictable "kick" or "put down" attempts to tell him or her what to do or how to behave—our *Structuring Response sets limits* in a nonjudgmental way. We *give information* about how actions hurt and injure. We *state what is important* and self-honoring. We *express concern*. We *give directives*. We state what is acceptable and not acceptable and why. We *confront hurtful behaviors*. We *guide*. We offer deep *values*. We suggest healthy, acceptable *choices*. We provide consequences. We show the way to get needs met. We are *consistent, potent,* and *believable*—in short, we offer tough love!

## STEPPING OFF THE DRAMA TRIANGLE

We can take our earlier scenario and see how it looks when the participants step off the Drama Triangle and respond instead from the Power Sharing Triangle.

WIFE: "You've got to take the dog to obedience school; she won't mind me." (*Victim*, looking for a *rescuer*, invites the other person into a *power play*.)

HUSBAND: "I hear you're having a hard time with the dog. I'm sorry for that." (*Nurturing Response*.) "I also hear you demanding me to take care of a problem that isn't mine." (*Structuring Response*.) "I need you to ask, not tell me, and give me the option to choose." (*Legitimate Need Response*.)

WIFE: "I'm having a difficult time in obedience training with our dog. Will you consider taking the dog to school?" (*Legitimate Need Response*.)

HUSBAND: "Thank you for asking me straight. I'd like to help you out, but I accepted your buying the dog with the understanding I would not be involved in the training. Also, I now have a commitment to build the deck and can't do both. Therefore I'll say no. But I'm willing to help you find a solution." (*Structuring Response*.)

After exploring family-of-origin issues, we can clearly see the unmet needs attempting to be met by stepping on the Drama Triangle. For the wife, it was a permission to be competent, to be powerful, to problem solve; for the husband, it was permission to have needs, to be treated as equal, and to say no. As they power shared, their talk was straight and their equality was affirmed.

### Power Dramas—A Constant Invitation

We have numerous invitations into power plays each day. To be self-honoring, we must step off and stay off the Drama Triangle. No easy task. We must wake up, see, feel, and hear the invitations to act powerless or more powerful. And from this we are called to create better endings, healthier options.

Power plays have the illusion of closeness. In contrast, power sharing allows you to experience a closeness that lets you stay on your path.

This brings out an important fact: We need both our masculine and our feminine energies. Power sharing is a *Structuring Response* that reflects our male energy, the positive use of our sword assertion. At the same time it is a *Nurturing Response*, one that responds to all that is feminine and encourages life and creativity. We need a healthy blend of both. Power sharing is a partnership model; power playing represents the competitive model. In power playing, we are likely to reexperience and reinforce negative traditions and the limiting authorities of the past. In power sharing, we create partnerships that merge love with power and power with love.

## CONCLUSION

None of us got everything we needed to power share easily. Power sharing must begin with empowering ourselves, knowing ourselves, and loving ourselves. This requires an honesty we may not like because it requires us to examine our human conditioning and to let go of false beliefs about power. It requires us to own our powerlessness over people and events that contain their own power.

In light of this, you can still take full responsibility for the pain you have inflicted upon yourself and others as you lived your life of illusion. The gifts will come as you replace control with trust, power plays with power sharing. You will begin to experience the powerful life energy you were intended to have, and the spiritual power will then flow through you. With practice, sharing in ways that empower you and affirm the power of others will become natural and freeing.

Here are ten skills that can be helpful to your process of moving from power plays to power sharing. Use them wisely and courageously each day.

1. Celebrate another's strengths when you are invited to be one-up; celebrate your own strengths when you are invited to be one-down.

2. Trust that you are an emotional and spiritual equal of others. Only your experiences and subsequent level of development are different.
3. Remember that who you are resides in your spiritual being and transcends your roles and your possessions.
4. Make judgments without being judgmental and let them pertain to yourself.
5. Decline the daily invitations that you encounter to be one-up or one-down.
6. Know that one-up and one-down are merely states of mind and not realities until you cooperate.
7. Stop personalizing another's thoughts, behaviors, and feelings.
8. Acknowledge that a person on a higher level of consciousness is equal to one on a lower level and is required to be patient and more yielding to the one on a lower level. A five-year-old child may know what it is like to be a two-year-old, but a two-year-old cannot know what it is like to be a five-year-old.
9. Think abundance. Power plays are based on scarcity thinking. Share what you have and what you do well.
10. Acknowledge that personal power is an inner resource you use to confidently be who you really are and do what you are in this world to do. It is not a commodity someone gives or takes away or one that gets you things.

To move closer to this goal of moving from power plays to power sharing, each day repeat the following affirmation: *I am a Radiant Child of the Universe. Divine Love, Wisdom, and Power, expressed through me, now bring to me all that I need to make my life complete.*

And now, wonder, instead of worry, about how power sharing will manifest itself in your life. Committed to the process of love, you can be sure that it will manifest.

You will then discover that power sharing is not just for your self-gratification or improving your love relationships. As we power share, we naturally bring our spiritual lover into a world that so badly needs it. This is the subject of our next chapter.

## ACTIVITY

### Signs of Power Sharing

Power sharing is a sign of healthy love. Because of life experiences that influenced us, we more easily power play than power share. In that regard, power plays can be our teacher. No doubt many of us have mastered power plays and no doubt we can also outgrow them.

Here is a list of ways of power sharing that support healthy love. Put a check by the qualities that easily appear in your life. Put an "X" by the characteristics that need special attention in your life.

_____ Being free to state beliefs, values, thoughts, and be heard and respected.

_____ Being free to express needs, wants, and feelings, and ask for support and love.

_____ Being free from ego-driven expectations and outcomes.

_____ Participating cooperatively to empower people in a positive way.

_____ Celebrating another's intelligence, knowledge, and other gifts; letting go of jealousy for what another has.

_____ Being willing to come out from your deepest self and interact with intimacy. Finding a meeting place where each person is willing to give and receive.

_____ Expressing personal power in a steady and reliable way. Being trustworthy and following through with promises.

_____ Giving of oneself in an emotionally supportive way without overnurturing. Just being there is enough.

_____ Compromising. Agreeing that we are emotional equals and each can take the lead sometimes.

_____ Mutual problem solving and decision making. Examining together how to do things more effectively.

_____ Owning and sharing mistakes guilt-free; making amends to self and others.

_____ Giving direct, clear answers to questions and requests.

_____ Taking actions that support equality and a win-win position. No one-up or one-down situations. Everyone is a winner.

_____ Accepting others where they are. Respecting the other person's being as you confront not-okay behaviors.

_____ Treating others with respect and sensitivity, especially when they are vulnerable.

_____ Having a solid sense of who we are and acknowledging the need to share ourselves with others.

_____ Listening, discussing, suggesting, and inviting, rather than telling, bribing, or threatening.

_____ Expressing anger and disappointment without the expectation of change. Letting go.

_____ Stopping verbal, emotional, and physical abuse in potent and respectful ways.

_____ Being assertive, not passive or aggressive.

_____ Sharing in making decisions and living with the outcomes.

_____ Being willing to yield or wait and accept not always getting what I want.

_____ Stating a position clearly, and respectfully letting go and trusting in positive outcomes.

## CHAPTER NINE

# Transforming the World

*For human character to reveal truly exceptional qualities, one must have the good fortune to be able to observe its performance over many years. If this performance is devoid of all egoism, if its guiding motive is unparalleled generosity, if it is absolutely certain that there is no thought of recompense and that, in addition, it has left its visible mark upon the earth, then there can be no mistake.*

*— Jean Giono*

The writer Jean Giono's stories are filled with remarkable heros: a shepherd, a venerable drunk, a storyteller, a hired hand. They are escorted by beasts and have knowledge of agriculture. In that solitude, they hear the voice of God. They experience creativity, freedom of expression, remorse for the destruction of life. In their wisdom, each exalted how human beings and nature itself live in harmony. Life is conserved and enriched, as humanity renews its ancient kinship with the earth.[1]

This quality of kinship with the earth is at the heart of spiritual loving. Here, spiritual love merged with power expands to embrace not only our partner but the entire human family. As we penetrate the illusion of separateness, we see that all humanity thinks with one mind and feels with one heart. The spiritual lover affirms the First Noble Truth of Buddhism—that all things suffer and desire freedom from suffering.

All of us are seeking health, happiness, wholeness. This is a process that transcends the boundaries of time, space, nation, and race.

It's possible to expand even from here. The spiritual lover can feel kinship with all living things and with the earth itself, the cradle of all things living. For the spiritual lover, this expansion occurs effortlessly. This is why I cannot draw a sharp line between love relationships and social action, community service, and ecology. All are manifestations of the spiritual lover that seeks to aid healing, wherever on the planet healing is needed.

Today nature calls for transformed people, for a new kind of being, for spiritual lovers of the earth. If we are alive, nature sees us as fit, having our own source of power. Nature strives toward balance and harmony. It has even been suggested that humans can use that power to live in a state of peace. In this state, we treat plant and animal life as a "thou" and respectfully thank it for its life, rather than slaughtering and pillaging life forms and treating them as objects.

Spiritual loving is no longer a luxury. If humanity is to survive, if the earth is to survive, we must expand our circles of compassion. This is the prime possibility of the 1990s and beyond—a possibility that transcends the theme of any decade we've yet experienced.

## THE THEMES OF FIVE DECADES

*The Fifties: Settling In.* The fifties were years of settling in after two world wars on either side of a major depression.

*The Sixties: Rebellion.* In our striving to not re-create the first half of the century, people in the sixties produced an era of rebellion. Anything there was to be against, many were. "Anti" rallies were everywhere. In our anti-war phase we abandoned our Vietnam veterans who were loyally living out the life of illusion, believing they were doing it right and returning to a world that remained in denial. They were shocked to come home to a world that not only failed to say welcome home, but pretended the war didn't exist or punished them for participating. Some are only now ready to trust and tell their horror stories.

*The Seventies: Independence.* The seventies moved us into a more gentle, but self-centered phase, that of independence. Here we began the focus on self: for example, searching for the right guru or therapist. Self-help books abounded. Though intended to be a temporary phase, for some, at least, this progressed into a way of life. "I" became more important than "you" or "we," as reflected in multiple partners, rampant divorce, fear of commitment, and codependency. Alcoholism, other drugs, sex, excitement—all became addictions. Women's movements and men's movements intensified.

*The Eighties: Better and Healthier Relationships.* Weary of the loud and lonely, the eighties quest was for better and healthier relationships. Adult children of alcoholics, family of origin, inner child, dysfunctional families, love addiction, and all our other addictions became pronounced themes. People said, "I want a healthier love, and I deserve it." Interdependency became the goal.

In the pattern of life, these five phases were necessary and important. Each phase showed us examples and extremes. Each made a statement. We needed rebellion to get past dependency. Like a two-year-old, however, we soon discovered temper tantrums and force didn't make it. And so, men and women alike began exploring their lives and began psychologically separating themselves from limiting influences of the past, a necessary step in becoming autonomous. From this independence came a natural progress to healthy belonging with others.

*The Nineties: Transformation.* As we enter the nineties, common themes are emerging: relating globally, creating a better world, getting ahold of the earth before it dies. Mechanistic, mind-over-matter thinking hasn't worked, nor has the "dominate or be dominated" mentality. Love with power is being called into action.

We have reason to be concerned. The forests of the world are disappearing. Our water, our air, our earth are all polluted. Species are disappearing. There are oil spills, landfills poisoning our drinking water, acid rain, and holes in the ozone layer. Natural habitats for birds and animals are plundered by developers after being okayed by "responsible" authorities.

The facts are disturbing. Fifteen million people, mostly children, die of starvation each year. Developing countries spend three times more on armaments than on health care. Poorer countries are diverting funds needed for development to fight drug traffic. One-third of humanity lacks safe drinking water. We take a forty-foot tree to produce a four-foot stack of newspaper.

In light of such facts, is there any question why we must wake up, get beyond the acquired learning, claim our true nature, and live it? For if we stop our self-search after just exploring our personal love relationships, then we too easily retreat into narcissism and miss the point of it all.

## CONSCIOUSNESS CONNECTS US TO ALL LIFE

The point is, we need to get ourselves together, our relationships working, to know the true meaning of love and power and to own it so we can share it in a world that really needs it. With our love and power working together, we do what really matters: We develop a *unity consciousness*, a way of seeing that connects us with *all* of life. We need to synthesize the best aspects of our human and spiritual lovers and, from that, walk into our daily life and create a different reality. It's not material world versus spiritual world. Pitting spirit against material is not the answer. Again, it's a connection with all of life. We have that potential partnership inside each of us, and that is the hope of the planet.

I once heard that only 5 percent of the world population needs this unity consciousness to change the consciousness of the world. When I first heard this I was excited. Wow! Only 5 percent? There's hope. But then I went into despair. You mean, there is not yet 5 percent of the world conscious? Who, or what, is running our planet? One of my students said, "If I'm being generous and assuming 5 percent of my colleagues are conscious, there may only be 1.7 aware people in the building where I work. No wonder I feel lonely at times."

Ken Keyes, Jr., tells the following story in his book, *The Hundredth Monkey*. Monkeys on a Japanese island were introduced to sweet potatoes. They liked the sweet potatoes but not the sand. One day an eighteen-month-old female monkey washed a sweet potato and discovered it tasted far better. She showed her mother and then she and her mother showed their friends. In a matter of six years, ninety-nine monkeys were washing their potatoes before they ate them. When the hundredth monkey did likewise, there was enough consciousness that it directed all monkeys on the island to wash their potatoes. It was then discovered that not only did monkeys on this island wash potatoes, but monkeys on another island were doing it as well.

The theme of this story is clear: *Consciousness thinking produces consciousness thinking.* We don't fully understand how or why. We only know that it does. Imagine a planet with 95 percent of its people living from unity consciousness. We could create a planet of exceeding richness and beauty, preserving it for generations. This, too, is our possibility.

## THE SPIRITUAL LOVER MOVING INTO THE WORLD

We are all called to the task. The spiritual person is not someone out there or up there—the mystic, the priest, the shaman, the medicine man. Spiritual people are those who are devoid of egoism and motivated by generosity, who have direct experience of their true nature, and who leave a mark on humanity. Spiritual love is in the millionaire who gives money to end world hunger and in the tinker man who collects cans to be recycled. This love is present in the man who fears commitment and the woman who believes she lacks power. The spiritual lover is in each of us if we want it. What we do know is that money can't buy spiritual love and poverty does not guarantee it. And addictions keep us from it.

The person who lives a life of spirit comes from the ranks of all ordinary people. He or she has synthesized the best aspects of that which is human and that which is spiritual. That person has a distinct character, a solidity called congruence—the insides and outsides match.

A spiritual lover is

- the woman who recycles not for a tax credit but because she is conscious.
- the man who eats less red meat, not only to lower cholesterol but because he cares about the rain forests.
- the woman who attempts to save the otter weighted with oil, and cries as it dies in her arms.

- the hunter who thanks and appreciates the animal, the game he seeks, and takes only that which is required to eat.
- the television anchorwoman who applauds community service daily on her newscast.
- the politician who talks about environmental issues from his soul and not based on the latest polls or Political Action Committee contribution.
- the environmentalist who is concerned because of her love and respect for the earth, not her resentment of the deteriorating quality of her life.
- the adventurer who travels the world to experience the various moods of Mother Nature.

Talking about relationships is but a beginning place. When we stay focused on relationships we are like a mouse, our nose so close to the ground we don't recognize what else is there. We must realize we are also the eagle, the bear, the owl, the wolf, and the other creatures of nature. As we begin stepping out of the relationship problem and own our love and power, we become like the eagle. Soaring high, we have a broader vision. To the Native American, the eagle is the power of the Great Spirit in each of us that calls us to balance the Earth and Spirit. The lofty eagle's view takes in both light and darkness.

### A Different Meaning to "Have To"

We cannot afford to "sleep," remain indifferent, unaware. "Asleep" we rationalize, avoid, project, despair: "It's too big for me; it's too scary to even think about." "What can I, one person, possibly do to make a difference?" "Someone else will figure out a solution; someone always has." If we remain "asleep," the end of the world as we know it may be at hand, and we may be caught unaware.

Some people in the early stages of recovery from love addiction have a difficult time giving. They are angered at suggestions that they contribute to the world at large. They hear it as a "have to," an obligation. While it is true we must take time to establish an autonomous self who can say no, we need to get beyond this point, to see on a spiritual level that there's a different meaning to "have to." This is not a matter of pleasing someone or being a "good" person; rather, caring for others and the world comes from the spiritual core. We recognize that we must take responsibility for what's happening.

Our possibility is to expand into the world as we experience our own transformation. Many people find this occurs naturally. After all, working on ourselves touches everyone we meet. This is inevitable, for we are connected to everything else, as Cindy discovered.

*Cindy's Story: "I was ready for outward expansion into doing."*

> In the process of all this inward gazing, I found myself feeling restless. I soon learned that the uneasiness was about a new personal truth: I was ready for outward expansion into doing. I found myself watching people and was drawn to goal setters, action takers, and change agents who had a noetic [based on intellect] quality. Observing others dispelled a subtle myth I'd been living: People who take action cannot be spiritual, and spiritual people cannot take action. The spell broken, I began to explore ways to take action in the world.

## THE NATURE OF CHANGE IN TODAY'S WORLD

Sociologist Pitirim Sorokin, with brilliant foresight, described a cyclical waxing and waning of three phases of cultural change: the *sensate*, the *ideational,* and the *idealistic.*[2] The *sensate* phase holds the material world as the ultimate reality. This is a world without spirituality, a world of matter over mind. Here, sensory perception is the source of knowledge and truth.

The *ideational* phase holds that truth lies beyond the material, in the spiritual realm. Knowledge is obtained through inner experience. It proposes superhuman standards and absolute ethical values. Judeo-Christian images of God and some forms of Eastern religion ascribe to this.

The interplay of these phases produces yet another, the *idealistic.* This third phase represents a harmonious blending of the first two. Reality is captured through both human and spiritual experience. Such cultures balance the aesthetic and technological, the biological and anthropological, the ecological and geological.

Our culture has been largely in the sensate phase. Our addictions, the desperate search to control pain, suffering, fear, and others, to seek answers outside of ourselves, to use power to control and dominate—all are reflections of such a phase. What is clear is that addictions and power plays are not working. Indeed, those who have confronted them have discovered that the flip side of addictions and power plays is life of spirit.

A dramatic shift is taking place. It is occurring more rapidly than any other transformation in the history of civilization. In short, though we are still heavily masculine, we are becoming more feminine.

### Living in Harmony with Change

With modern technologies—computers, TVs, satellite communication—bits of new knowledge are bombarding us at incredible rates. Change is happening faster than we ever dreamed possible. Part of the problem we face is that we resist the inevitable: change. Life is change; change is life. Movement is natural and spontaneous. The cultural transformation is happening.

And change is uncomfortable. God forbid we be uncomfortable. That's why we turn to our old habits even when they are destructive. We want to control, deny, outwit, or, simply put, power play with nature. We can minimize the pain of this by recognizing chaos as a necessary part of evolution in all of life. Spring follows winter, winter follows fall, and fall follows summer. Try as we can, we cannot stop that phenomenon.

What continues to amaze me is how audacious mankind has become to think it can control life with its mind. Rather than fighting change forced on us, we can live in harmony with it. We can say good-bye to outdated beliefs about "man's" domination over the earth. We can thank those aspects of life for what they have provided and let them be teachers, a leading edge to the new.

Major transformations are occurring all over the globe. It's a time of Yin, where we can understand the true meaning of the female principle of passivity as it calls us to work in harmony with change and stop working against it. For active, aggressive *male* Yang cultures, this will be a challenge of huge proportions indeed! Will we get it? Will we stop the illusion of neighborly love and truly share power throughout the world? Many nations have an illusion of power and one-upmanship. On the Drama Triangle, they need other nations to rescue and persecute.

None of the Yang values pursued in cultures are intrinsically bad. It's in isolating them from their polar opposite, Yin, that we have and will continue to fail. Our leaders need to seek counsel, not only from scientists, but from the poets, the philosophers, the spiritual teachers. We need the best aspects of science and technology, the material world to protect Mother Earth and all of her inhabitants. She is our life sustenance. We can use a sword to cut off what injures her, not to destroy her.

It's time we identify with the whole organism and take ownership of our follies. We must be willing to let Mother Earth be both nurturing and uncontrollable. What seems clear is that overemphasis on science and rational thinking has nearly obliterated our planet. It is anti-ecological. We must, if we are to survive, combine them with the intuitive wisdom known throughout history and, for us, most directly in our Native American cultures.

In a material sense, it is time to share what we know in a partnership. In power sharing we all win. In power playing we continue to lose. What would the world be like if we distributed the wealth of the planet equally and operated from our spiritual lover? Not only our relationships but our world would be transformed.

## Change Calls Us to Become Conscious

The encounter with birth and death are major themes in life. It may be the experience of death of a loved one, a relationship, a career, a role, an addiction, a phase of life. All mythology speaks to this. As we've learned, facing these crises forces us to examine how we can live life more fully.

Carlos Castaneda, author of *Journey to Ixtlan*, quoted his spiritual guide, Don Juan: "An immense amount of pettiness is dropped if your death makes gesture to you, or if you have glimpses of it. Death is the only wise advisor that we have." What stance would you take in life if you knew your death was taking place tomorrow?

Perhaps, in facing ecological crisis and war, we are taking death as our advisor on a planet-wide scale. If so, then we are more willing to look at life from a much broader perspective. If I sound pessimistic,

I don't intend to be. In truth I am hopeful. I'm not certain whether the changes that are occurring are because our learned self fears death, or if it's because we are more spiritually awake. Is it scarcity thinking or spirit speaking? Probably both.

Perhaps the call of death is part of both personal and cultural transformation that are occurring in the world at large. Perhaps our arrogance is meeting us face-on as we experience the ecological crisis. The nations of Eastern Europe learned that without food their people die, so they began transforming their economic systems so more food could be produced. Similarly, the only way to resolve the existential crisis is to transcend it by owning the illusions that created it and seeing them as lessons to grow from. It calls us to be aware—to step into our spiritual lover, the eagle in us, and take a broader view of life.

### Why Consciousness Is the Solution

The solution to our ecological crisis lies in a wider consciousness—that is, in our ability to see the world with unity consciousness. At no time in history have we been asked to change so rapidly. The time calls first for us to wake up to that consciousness, to have enough self-love to claim the personal and spiritual power needed to create our own meaning. As we become aware of our oneness with all life, we can begin to love, guide, and educate our children with consciousness. We learn to share power with our partner, with our society, with our earth.

The problem is that we have years of acquired learning to overcome and transcend. And since the changes are upon us now, we have a responsibility to act *now*. Though we may not be able to release all that blocks us, we can, in being awake, own our learned self, our messes, and our contribution to the demise of self, relationships, and earth.

Conscious, real, awake, we are free to see who we are, what we're really doing, why we're doing it. If we don't like it, we change it. We operate from an inside set of values, rules based on intrinsic truth; we no longer are controlled by rules established for the masses. We stop hurting ourselves, others, and the earth, because it's wrong to hurt and it's right to stop. We operate from regret and remorse and no longer are run by guilt and shame. Coming from our spiritual lover, we cannot help but be a part of creating a better world.

## The Earth Is Alive

*The President in Washington sends word that he wishes to buy our land. But how can you buy or sell the sky? The land? The idea is strange to us. If we do not own the freshness of the air and the sparkle of the water, how can you buy them?*

*Every part of this earth is sacred to my people. Every shining pine needle, every sandy shore, every mist in the dark woods, every meadow, every humming insect. All are holy in the memory and experience of my people. . . .*

*If we sell you our land, you must remember that it is sacred.*

— Chief Seattle's letter of 1852 responding to the
United States government's request to buy land

*Gaia* is the name the Greeks used for the Earth Goddess. It is also the name James Lovelock gives to his idea that the earth is alive, is a living whole.[3] That it is actively maintained and regulated.

We have veered away from this ancient concept. The focus has been on seeing the earth as rock and keeping it separate from life.

The *Gaia* Theory stresses the interrelationship between the earth and life; the planet earth is alive. The rocks, the air, the oceans, the dirt on which we walk—each is as much a part of life as the living creatures. As Lovelock wrote, "Life and its environment are so closely coupled that evolution concerns *Gaia,* not the organisms or the environment taken separately. . . . Thinking of the earth as alive makes it seem, on happy days, in the right place, as if the whole planet were celebrating a sacred ceremony."

A *Gaia* perspective forces us to think in a broader planetary scope. People who are concerned about the environment only for its impact on human life fail to see the point. It's self-serving, mechanistic. Our spiritual lover calls us to respect all of that which contributes to the greater harmony of the universe. We must speak and care about the earth out of reverence for it and not so it can serve us better. Primitive rituals and Native American ceremonies reflected this interrelatedness.

## One Society Living in Harmony with the Earth

We have both the potential and the responsibility to create a civilization that combines love and power, the feminine and masculine principles, the inner and outer realities, the spiritual and material worlds. What would a society, bearing the marks of the natural human condition, look like?

Perhaps it is no more brilliantly exemplified than among the San of the Kalahari Desert, a simple society studied extensively by anthropologists for twenty-five years, as described in *The Tangled Wings* by Melvin Konner.[4] That study captured the essence of a life that shattered beliefs about human nature.

The San lived in organic harmony with the world and each other. Their knowledge of plant and animal life was astounding. Though this knowledge provided them a way to live, their knowledge went far beyond what was needed for survival. Women gathered fruits, nuts, vegetables. Three-fourths of the food their families needed to stay alive came from the gathering. The San hunters provided fresh meat. They killed only what was needed, and game populations remained in balance. They had deep respect and fascination with animals. Courage and bravery were widespread. Women saw being pregnant with a first child as a transforming event and created rituals to celebrate that event with other women.

The organic harmony experienced in nature extended to human relationships as well. Conflicts were resolved by talking in groups, sometimes for hours. The true meaning of the encounter marathon was here. A frank expression of feelings began at dusk and sometimes continued all night. Voices were loud, yet equality universal. No social or economic distinctions were evident. The ethic of sharing was so powerful that miserliness (selfishness) was ranked as the number one sin. Violence was considered a mental disorder. All food gathered was equally shared. The first word many of the children learned was "give."

The ethic of power sharing, mutual interdependency, and organic harmony was vividly expressed in the trance/dance ritual, an impassioned drama of healing. The mystery of wholeness was expressed as both sacred and human, and engendered energy needed by the healers to confront death itself. As the sick lay by the fire, their loved ones were nearby. Women encircled the fire and sang songs that brought them together into another level of consciousness. Inspired, the men danced the circle. Life and death counted on this mutuality.

The experience of the San defies primitive human groups as solitary, poor, brutal, ignorant. Far from solitary, it is a partnership exemplified: a balance of male and female energies. Far from poor, it is abundant. Far from brutality, it abounds with mutual respect, generosity, love. Far from ignorant, it is civilized and philosophical. The elderly are cared for, not sent to a high-rise ghetto or a nursing home. They are surrounded by loving grandchildren and adults who are not afraid to show them courtesy. Though imperfect, the culture of the San affirms what we are capable of.

## TAKING LOVE AND POWER INTO THE WORLD

*Only if we have a beautiful world, can we have a beautiful mind and a beautiful soul.*

— *Father Thomas Berry*

Our three lovers respond differently to the earth. The addictive lover uses the earth to self-gratify. With greed and biotechnology, we alter the makeup of the world so it will serve us. The healthy lover is ecologically aware, concerned, and oftentimes becomes an activist. The spiritual lover goes one step further and sees the sacredness in each animal, in each tree. Birds, wind, clouds—all are voices to awaken us to the deeper mysteries of life. Nature activates our sensitivities. Poetry, altered states of consciousness, reverence for the earth evolve.

If human beings were to disappear from earth, the *Gaia*, the totality of life, would go on. How is it that human beings think the earth is here to be controlled? We must see the human species and other species as a total community. We must see habitat—all habitat—as sacred.

Morality has for too long been concerned with suicide, homicide, genocide. It has neglected biocide and geocide (organism and earth killers, respectively). Until we include these last two, our morality is collapsing.

It is not enough to focus on ourselves, to just take care of us, to have healthier relationships for us. That is the ego speaking. We must establish a human presence in the natural world that views the planet as our physical, biological, relational, and spiritual home. We cannot have healthy people or healthy love on a sick planet.

## WE CAN CREATE A WORLD THAT WORKS

*Each second we live in a new and unique moment of the universe, a moment that never was before and will never be again. And what do we teach our children in school? We teach them that two and two make four; and that Paris is the capital of France. When will we also teach them what they are? We should say to each of them: Do you know what you are? You are a marvel. You are unique. In all of the world there is no other child like you. . . . You have the capacity for anything. Yes, you are a marvel. And when you grow up, can you then harm another who is, like you, a marvel? You must cherish one another. You must work—we must all work—to make this world worthy of its children.*

— *Pablo Casals*
*from* Joys and Sorrows

Although we can learn from the San culture, we cannot go back in time. Imitating the gatherer and hunter is not the answer. We can no longer be nomads nor can we afford to throw away technology. What we can do is return to an organic way of living that leads to a saner world. The sane world is a conscious world. It knows the true meaning of love as giving, power as sharing. It knows living in peace is a natural phenomena, and war unnatural. It is where the chalice and the blade, the masculine and feminine link. Harmony is the experience.

We can create a workable world. Our biology knows it, our history gives evidence of it. Our psyche has the potential to do so. Our spiritual lover doesn't question it. We can live spiritually within the constraints of our biology. We must. The adaptations we make to cope, survive grief, face death, belong with another, become psychological constraints. Hiding our grief, masking fears, retreating from touch, withholding love are, without question, as possible in our biological makeup as are generously loving and sharing our power.

We've learned that it is the influences in our history that limit our human potential and spirit. We can surpass these learned limitations that confused us about love and power and once again experience a conscious and enlightened self. When we do so, men and women living in partnership will translate into the larger world: enlightened families, schools, governments, nations. Linking will replace ranking. Flexibility will replace rigidity. Technology will return to the pride of creativity and craftmanship—carpentry, pottery, weaving. Management will play life-supporting roles, freeing us to actualize our creative potential. Production will encourage worker participation.

As we move from domination to partnership in our relationships, and balance masculine and feminine energies, the danger of nuclear annihilation will gradually diminish. Conscious utilization of our natural resources and individual population control will eliminate the necessity of famine, war, disease. Power sharing will impact the environment as it replaces conquest of nature with love of nature.

Abundance thinking will make poverty and hunger memories. Suicide, vandalism, addiction, child abuse, homicide, terrorism, will be a surprise if they appear in our daily news. National and international affairs will improve. Some of the best aspects of communism and capitalism will merge into a new meaning of democracy. Our economic system will be directed by conscious men and women. Our self-help books will guide us to living harmoniously with the planet, support our growth, and give ways to achieve healthier love and power sharing.

Man will now be free to own the feminine and no longer fear castration. He will be free to love. Woman, open to her masculine and caring for herself, will no longer fear abandonment. Healthy love will be the norm. Conscious parents will bond with their children, teaching trust, giving, and power sharing. A renewed celebration of love will include a healthier expression of sexual pleasure, friendship. All caring, loving relationships will be recognized. Religion will affirm our spiritual evolution. Myth will again speak directly to the soul and continue to help us synthesize our psychological and spiritual energies.

Above all, we will return to unity consciousness. We will return to the sacred, to a meaningful spiritual ritual that tells us what we already know: *We are all one under the sun.*

## ACTIVITIES

### 1. *Experiencing Healing Rituals*

Our addictions and preoccupation with self-gratification not only destroy ourselves and our relationships, but the earth itself has been abused, ignored, minimized, made to seem unimportant in the eyes of people. We need a ritual of atonement to transform our remorse for practices that have harmed the earth. We must acknowledge our part of the ecological mess. We must not, however, judge too harshly or become depressed over what's happened. Many have been asleep to what's been taking place and in our false dependency, believed someone else would take care of the messes we made of our earth. If you don't know what you're doing, you are innocent. Once you know, once awake, and you continue, you lose your innocence.

Let's celebrate the earth and honor it with rituals of the sacred moments—each sunrise, sunset, each solstice. Redemption can come to mean a celebration, entering the joy after learning of the chaos.

Rituals are important parts of our transformational process. They speak to us at an emotional and soul level. They symbolically mark the movement from one life phase to another. They bond us with important events. They call witness to our growth. They both ground and heal.

Via our negative learnings we have been users and takers of our planet. It is important we give back.

The task is this: Take a seed, a seedling, some plant form. Go into nature. Let your intuitive nature find a special spot. Dig a hole in the earth and give it all the negative thoughts, feelings, and actions that have prevented you from being a spiritual lover with you, others, and the earth. Spend time here. Cry or yell if you need to.

This ritual can be a powerful emotional release and can facilitate a spiritual bonding with yourself and the earth. When done, cover the hole. Thank the earth for all it has done. Take time here.... Dig another hole and plant what you brought as a symbol of the transformed attitudes, actions that will guide you. State these.

If this is a place you can frequent, do so, nourish the plant. Watch it grow. Let it be a metaphor for your personal transformation. What follows is an activity that encourages you to actualize your spiritual lover in the world.

## 2. Saving the Earth

Here is a random list of thirty-five things you can do for planetary consciousness. Put a check by those you are *in the habit of doing*. If you find you don't have enough of these good habits, begin to form new ones today. Be a role model. It doesn't matter if you begin doing what's right from the outside in. If you recycle under pressure instead of doing it with consciousness, eventually you will get it! As a habit develops, at some point it will become your consciousness.

1. Buy recyclables, recycle them, and buy products made from recyclables. (We use 2.5 million plastic bottles an hour in the United States.)
2. Drive a fuel-efficient automobile and keep it in top shape. Rotate tires regularly for maximum tire life, and maintain proper air pressure for fuel efficiency.
3. Use public transportation whenever possible or share rides.
4. Eat lower on the food chain—vegetables, fruits, grains.
5. Hang your clothes in the sun and wind to dry when possible.
6. Turn down the heat; turn up the temperature at which the air conditioner kicks on or do without one.
7. Use less water when you shower, do dishes, shave, brush teeth. Hand wash your car.
8. Save batteries. Recycle batteries when possible. Use rechargeable batteries.
9. Join a credible environmental organization.
10. Use ventilation and plants to freshen air, especially in airtight offices.
11. Use organic fertilizers on lawns, in gardens. Use predator insects for insect control, or attract birds to do the job.
12. Plant at least one tree per year and nurture it to be sure it survives.
13. Write letters to business, media people, and politicians who are actively concerned about the environment.
14. Ask your grocer to return to paper bags for vegetables and fruits, *or* bring your own.
15. Use the telephone—do preliminary shopping by phone; it saves not only automobile fuel but your energy too!

16. Conserve paper and use paper products rather than plastics.
17. Do what you can to *stop* the two million tons of junk mail sent each year.
18. Return to Grandma's cleaning basics—vinegar, soda, ammonia, pumice stones, cornstarch, biodegradable soaps, Borax, and newspaper.
19. Limit the amount of plastics you use—one way is to use cloth diapers.
20. Write your concerns to your congressperson.
21. Never litter! Tell people you are offended/concerned when you see them abuse the environment.
22. Be concerned about groundwater contamination. Ground water is half of our water supply.
23. Preserve and create a wildlife refuge or bird sanctuary in your own yard.
24. Hunt and gather only that which you will eat.
25. Make routine times to appreciate nature. You will nourish and protect what you savor.
26. Think "small is beautiful and abundant." Build smaller, more efficient homes and businesses. Change attitudes that support big and new is better.
27. Read, read, read! Educate yourself to what is happening. Remember: Ignorance is not bliss! It's ignorance.
28. Bring a ceramic mug to work instead of using and throwing away Styrofoam cups.
29. Use linen towels instead of paper napkins.
30. Carry an expandable shopping bag.
31. Think long term. Convenience may be a dead end.
32. Educate yourself to be an environmentally sound shopper.
33. Give environmentally sound gifts.
34. Do what you can to preserve the world's forests.
35. Think about world population and consider limiting the number of children you have—or having no children.

# Epilogue

The voice came from nowhere, or so it seemed. I was in a room talking to my partner and friend; the TV news was blaring in the background. The voice, vaguely familiar, said, *Brenda, it's time to stop pretending your life is ordinary!* The words went through me like a blade. I had direct experience of the meaning. Everything stopped. I was opened.

That morning I had had a phone interview. I was introduced as a well-known author and psychologist. I chuckled to myself and tried to minimize that introduction. After all, I had once been told that visibly owning my talents is a sin of pride.

The voice went on and said, "You are not required to do anything more. There is no such thing as 'have to.' But what you are doing and not doing, take responsibility for. Know there is more you can do. It is your fear that stops you. Own your fear. Then decide to do or not to. And do so with absolute honesty!"

The message was powerful. I could not stop crying. I assured my partner and friend that what was going on with me was beyond him and in some way beyond me.

I took several weeks to examine fully, to feel intensely, each of my fears. I knew what I feared was likely to happen, as I stopped viewing my life as ordinary, as I agreed to take responsibility for my talents and fully commit to my spiritual path.

With full knowledge of my fears, I accepted the knowledge of who I am and agreed to enter fully the next phase of my life.

I am in it. What I feared would happen has for the most part happened. There are times I rebel, I doubt, I want to retreat. There is no going back. And though I'm not sure where walking my path this time will take me, I am willing to trust the voice. Listening to that inner knowing, I do not fail myself or my relationships.

Remarkable things have already happened to me as I've tried to live out these words. Writing this book has been a part of it. I have shared only a small bit of knowledge and theories that excite me and support me in my own path of transformation. What I've shared is intended more to stimulate your thirst than to quench it.

The intent is to help us recognize the following points:

- *We are both one and many.* Various lovers, each with its own way of experiencing the world, are inside us. Most important for understanding our relationships are three selves we move in and out of: the learned self, the autonomous self, and the spiritual self.

- *The **learned self** views love as a commodity.* It says our prime task is to live life as influenced by others who love us or whose love we desire. The learned self adapts to make itself safe and predictable even when love is not there. Power is played with—hoarded or suppressed. Control and domination are evident. We are either one-up or one-down and rarely equal. This way of seeing the world becomes the hallmark of the *addictive lover.* It stresses *having* —taking care of others at our own emotional expense, or possessing the "right person" as an emotional fix to ward off unhappiness. Sometimes, in fear, the addictive lover stays on the edge of love. It has a warped view of what masculine and feminine mean.

  Our challenge is to unmask the edicts of the learned self, seeing that they were based on decisions we made when we viewed ourselves largely as powerless children in a world of giants. Only then can we see how those decisions generate the shame, guilt, and anger that cripple our relationships in the present.

- *Having the courage to know, we give birth to the **autonomous self.*** Here, love is claimed freely without suppressing our personal power. We relate to each other as emotional equals in a world where there is enough love and power for everyone. We can meet our needs by developing an inner mother and father or asking directly for what we need.

  This is the view of the *healthy lover,* who knows it is safe to think, feel, and act the way we choose, while also considering the needs of others. The healthy lover knows that it is important for man and woman to develop the best aspects of their feminine and masculine qualities, to form partnerships where love and power coexist.

- *Yet something more is possible for us, something even beyond autonomy and the healthy lover.* We can gain access to our *spiritual self* that knows a deeper meaning of love and power; a self that can transform not only our relationships but our lives as we tap into knowledge waiting to be recognized.

  The spiritual self believes in abundance and experiences love and power as our true nature. Personality is simply a tool to express our spiritual nature. As we experience this truth we know the miracle of who we are—*spiritual lovers.* As spiritual lovers, we develop an eagle's-eye view of our history and work with fundamental laws of transformation. As we fully accept that the process of change is the only constant in relationships, we transcend our problems and place no conditions on the people we love. We see relationships as sacred events, the people we love (and sometimes dislike) as teachers, and each moment of our life as something to savor. In our relationships we finally marry love and power. Our love expands so that we feel kinship with all living beings, including the earth. We feel a unity consciousness embracing all life.

There is so much exciting to know about your possibilities. I encourage you to listen to the spiritual lover within your body and psyche, to passionately affirm its right to be and fill it with the food of knowledge, experience, and love. As you listen to the quiet place within you, you will know how to, and which people, support your evolution and the evolution of the planet.

Take your personal power. Walk more of the earth, feel the land. Hear the birds, marvel at the plants, respect the four-legged brothers and sisters. Connect with all the elements of the earth and the life they support.

As I reflect on the message I received, I recognize it's time to pass it on. To you I say, Stop pretending your life is ordinary, for it is not! You are not required to do any more than you are already doing. But whatever you are doing or not doing, take full responsibility for. Examine your fears. If you can, transcend them. Discover the mystery of your wholeness, the spiritual lover in you. Then, decide for yourself what you will do and not do in all of your love relationships. There is a warrior in you, a hero and heroine capable of merging love with power and carrying it into the world. *We are all descendants of great hunters and gatherers.*

Like holograms, we reflect energy. And what we reflect, reflects back to us. Do you like what you see? If not, do something—now.

Yes, you deserve love and power. More importantly, you are love and power. Stop waiting and discover them, live them, share them now. We will all benefit.

Peace, love, courage.

# APPENDIX

The following lists first appeared in my book, *Is It Love or Is It Addiction?*

## CHARACTERISTICS OF THE ADDICTIVE LOVER

Addictive lovers can have several of the following characteristics.

- They feel consumed.
- They have difficulty defining ego boundaries.
- They often exhibit sadomasochism.
- They fear letting go.
- They fear risk, change, and the unknown.
- They experience little individual growth.
- They have difficulty experiencing true intimacy.
- They play psychological games.
- They give to get something back.
- They attempt to change the other.
- They need the other to feel complete.
- They seek solutions outside the self.
- They demand and expect unconditional love.
- They refuse or abuse commitment.
- They look to others for affirmation and worth.
- They fear abandonment when routinely separated.
- They recreate familiar, negative feelings.
- They desire, yet fear, closeness.
- They attempt to take care of others' feelings.
- They power play.

## CHARACTERISTICS OF THE HEALTHY LOVER

People in healthy relationships have the following characteristics.

- They allow for individuality.
- They experience both oneness with and separateness from a partner.
- They bring out the best qualities in a partner.
- They accept endings.
- They experience openness to change and exploration.
- They invite growth in the other partner.
- They experience true intimacy.
- They feel the freedom to ask honestly for what is wanted.
- They experience giving and receiving in the same way.
- They do not attempt to change or control the other.
- They encourage self-sufficiency in self and partner.

- They accept limitations of self and partner.
- They do not seek unconditional love.
- They accept and respect commitment.
- They have a high self-esteem.
- They trust the memory of the beloved. They enjoy solitude.
- They express feelings spontaneously.
- They welcome closeness and risk vulnerability.
- They care with detachment.
- They affirm equality and personal power of self and partner.

## CHARACTERISTICS OF POWER PLAYS

The transition from childish omnipotence to power sharing seems to be something we all struggle with in childhood and adolescence, even in adult life. Confusion over the uses of power is evident in unhealthy, uneasy adult relationships. What are some of the power plays that sabotage adult lover relationships?

- Giving advice but not accepting it
- Having difficulty in reaching out and in asking for support and love
- Giving orders; demanding and expecting much from others
- Trying to "get even" or to diminish the self-esteem or power of others
- Being judgmental; put-downs that sabotage others' success; faultfinding; persecuting; punishing
- Holding out on others; not giving what others want or need
- Making, then breaking promises; causing others to trust us and then betraying the trust
- Smothering, overnurturing the other
- Patronizing, condescending treatment of the other that sets one partner up as superior and the other as inferior; intimidation
- Making decisions for the other; discounting the other's ability to solve problems
- Putting the other in no-win situations
- Attempting to change the other (and unwillingness to change the self)
- Attacking the other when he or she is most vulnerable
- Showing an antidependent attitude: "I don't need you"
- Using bullying, bribing behavior; using threats
- Showing bitterness, self-righteous anger, or holding grudges
- Abusing others verbally, physically, or emotionally
- Being aggressive and defining it as assertiveness
- Needing to win or be right
- Resisting stubbornly or being set in one's own way
- Having difficulty admitting mistakes or saying "I'm sorry"
- Giving indirect, evasive answers to questions
- Defending any of the behaviors on this list

# ENDNOTES

## CHAPTER ONE
### Love, Power, and Transformation

1. P. D. Ouspensky, *In Search of the Miraculous: Fragments of an Unknown Teaching* (New York: Harcourt Brace Jovanovich, 1965).

## CHAPTER TWO
### Love and Power in Crisis

1. From "Education Update," Minnesota Department of Education, vol. 23, no. 2 (October 1988). Laura Kiscaden, specialist in sex desegregation, references a survey of sixth to ninth graders in Rhode Island. One-half said a woman walking alone, dressed seductively, is asking to be raped; one-third said it is not wrong for a man to rape a woman with previous sexual experience; 65 percent of males and 47 percent of females okayed date rape; and 87 percent of males and 79 percent of females said rape is okay in marriage. The author attributes the problem to cultural stereotyping.

2. Helen E. Fisher, in her work *The Sex Contract* gives evidence of how the changing of the female estrous cycle periodicity affects relationships. Psychological fears of abandonment and engulfment may contribute to inequities in love and power.

3. Riane Eisler's work *The Chalice and the Blade* thoroughly reviews changes over the past five thousand years that have contributed to the polarization of feminine and masculine.

4. Medieval history as shown in *The Art of Courtly Love* by Capellanus; *The Power of Myth,* an interview of Joseph Campbell by Bill Moyers; and numerous other chronicles and stories in literature—all demonstrate how the search for a balance of the masculine and feminine was often experienced in a mystical form of romantic love.

5. The sources of the role of religion I used are numerous: personal experience and talks with spiritual teachers and clients; Joseph Campbell's talks with Bill Moyers; Gerda Lerner's *The Creation of Patriarchy;* Matthew Fox's *Original Blessing,* pages 9 and 101; and Marilyn French's *Beyond Power,* Chapter 2.

6. Gerda Lerner, *The Creation of Patriarchy,* 172-73.

7. Matthew Fox, *Original Blessing,* 309.

8. Sarah, the wife of Abraham, conceived and had a son, Isaac, at age ninety-nine. This brought joy and celebration (Gen. 21:1-8). Jacob had a dream in which there was a stairway that reached from earth to heaven and God. (Gen. 28:10-22). Metaphorically, the birth/dance (as in the story of Sarah) can represent the life-giving feminine principle; the ladder/stairway (Jacob's dream) can symbolize the masculine principle or the power to transcend our ego and seek spiritual truth.

9. Phyllis Chesler and Emily Goodman first mentioned twelve power bases for women and men in *Women, Money, Power*, 273.

10. From an article "Some Mothers May Not Give Dads a Chance," *Minneapolis Star and Tribune* (10 January 1988), by Kim Ode. The author references Frances Grossman's five and one-half year study of twenty-three families.

11. Robert Bly workshop, Oaxtapec, Mexico, January 1990.

12. Additional information I have used to support psychological perspectives data comes from many sources. Most important are the hundreds of developmental stories I have heard in my therapy and workshop practice. Other sources: developmental theories; *Father-Daughter Incest*, by Judith Herman; *Men Who Rape* by A. Nicholas Groth; "A Food Fix" lecture by Sandra Gordon Stoltz; "Today's Troubled Men," by Herbert J. Freudenberger, *Psychology Today* (December 1987); "Women Batterers: The Sins of Our Brothers," by David Adams, *Sojourners* (May 1982); *Time* article on the Hite Report (12 October 1987).

## CHAPTER THREE
### Healing: From Script to Autonomy

1. From Eric Berne's *What Do You Say after You Say Hello?*, 33.

2. Ibid., 213.

3. Ibid.,106.

4. G. I. Gurdjieff, modern spiritual teacher, taught that each person has a chief feature around which the delusions of self revolve. He introduced the Enneagram theory that proposes nine personality types. As we become conscious and transcend our life scripts, we express the virtue of the best qualities of our personality type. But when we are under stress, we disintegrate and express vice or the negative tendencies of our personality type. Compassionate understanding of our personality type and the personality types of those we relate to can reduce the amount of needless suffering in relationships. Helen Palmer in *The Enneagram* and Don Richard Riso in *Personality Types* and *Understanding the Enneagram* address personality types in detail.

5. The positions described were original to Taibi Kahler in "The Mini Script" article written in conjunction with Hedges Capers that appeared in *Transactional Analysis Journal* 4:1 (January 1974). An updated version of this theory can be found in the book *Transactional Analysis Revisited*, 234-48. For simplification and to emphasize the theme of the book, I have utilized the four original positions: Driver, Stopper, Vengeful, and Payoff in the learned self. The Driver information is original to Dr. Kahler. I have added Robert L. Goulding and Mary McClure Goulding's injunction theory to demonstrate the Stopper Position. To the third position, Vengeful, I have added the power plays described in my previous book, *Is It Love or Is It Addiction?*

6. Additional information on script injunctions can be found in Mary McClure Goulding and Robert L. Goulding's *Changing Lives Through Redecision Therapy*, 34-43. The most current information on injunctions can be found in their book *Not To Worry*.

7. Berne, *What Do You Say after You Say Hello?*, 137-39. Rackets are now thought to be a composite of distorted feelings supported by internal beliefs and memories and manifested in external behaviors, as described by Richard Erskine and Marilyn J. Zalcman in "Rackets and Other Treatment Issues," *Transactional Analysis Journal* 9:1 (January 1979).

8. Hedges Capers suggested to Taibi Kahler that he focus on the Okay Autonomy Positions. Capers identified and labeled the four Okay Miniscript Positions. See "The Miniscript," *Transactional Analysis Journal* 4:1 (January 1974).

9. Permissions are messages that affirm what is within us and our right to act upon it. References: Annette Bodmer, *The Gift of Affirmations* (Savage, Minn.: Affirmations Enterprises, 1985); Jean Illsley Clarke, *Self-Esteem: A Family Affair* (Minneapolis: Winston Press, 1978); Pamela Levin, *Becoming the Way We Are*, 1974; Brenda Schaeffer, "Corrective Parenting" chart, 1981.

## CHAPTER FOUR
### Transformation: From Autonomy to Spirituality

1. The main source of pages 93-95: "History of Psychology," American Psychological Association exam materials; Fritjof Capra, *The Turning Point*, Chapters 2 and 6.

2. Fritjof Capra, *The Turning Point*.

3. William Blake, from "Auguries of Innocence," *Anthology of Romanticism*, 3rd ed. rev., Ernest Bernbaum, ed. (New York: The Ronald Press Company, 1948), 132.

4. Chapter 8 of *The Thirteen Petalled Rose* by Adin Steinsaltz discusses the essence of Jewish existence and the meaning of repentance as a return to self.

## CHAPTER FIVE
### The Spiritual Lover in You

1. Joseph Campbell speaks to this in his interview with Bill Moyers in *The Power of Myth*.

## CHAPTER SIX
### Laws of Transformation

1. No one human source can be credited for these laws. They have been identified in traditional spiritual schools and in physics. They have been

addressed in numerous books and by numerous teachers and authors, some of which are The I Ching, Old and New Testament, Fourth Way School of Development, Joseph Weed in *Wisdom of the Mystic Masters, A Course in Miracles,* Fritjof Capra in *The Turning Point,* Jacquelyn Small in *Transformers— The Therapists of the Future.*
2. Fritjof Capra, *The Turning Point,* 41, and referencing Arthur Koestler's *Janus.*

### CHAPTER SEVEN
### Love as a Process

1. J. L. Schiff, author of *The Cathexis Reader,* identified four levels of discounts that support four passive behaviors: (1) do nothing, (2) overadapt to others, (3) agitation, and (4) incapacitation or violence. In the four discounts, we can discount the problem by denying it exists, minimizing its importance, believing it is unresolvable, or discounting ourselves or others by making a person greater or less than they are. Note: Anytime we recognize and accept the discount we have entered an addictive or codependent relationship— unhealthy symbiosis.
2. The rubberband theory was first referenced by David Kupfer and Morris Haimowitz, *Transactional Analysis Journal* 1:1 (1971) 10-16.

### CHAPTER EIGHT
### Power Sharing

1. Stephen Karpman, M.D., is a Teaching Member of the International Transactional Analysis Association. He won the Eric Berne Memorial Award for his Drama Triangle Model in 1972. The simplicity and clarity can be helpful to recognizing games in process. For this book, I have used the power plays to refer to games that involve a struggle for power. In my opinion, all games indicate a belief in inequities of power. Reference: "Fairy Tales and Script Drama Analysis," *Transactional Analysis Bulletin* 7:26 (April 1968) 40, 41.
2. The theory of the Power Sharing Triangle and its three positions is original to me. The idea of superimposing the Power Sharing Triangle over the Drama Triangle is original to student and colleague David A. Larson, Licensed Psychologist.

### CHAPTER NINE
### Transforming the World

1. Jean Giono, *The Man Who Planted Trees,* as described by Norma L. Goodrich, Claremont, Calif., May 1985.

2. The source of information on Pitirim Sorokin is Fritjof Capra, *The Turning Point*, 31, which references *Social and Cultural Dynamics* by Sorokin, 4 vols., New York: American Book Company, 1937-1941.

3. James Lovelock in *The Ages of Gaia* views the earth as a coherent system of life and notes that the stresses present on earth are man-made. He emphasizes geo-physiology as he bridges geology and physiology. Organisms and rocks have a relationship.

4. Chapter 1, *The Tangled Wing* by Melvin Konner draws additionally on the works of Lee and DeVore, Marshall, Howell and Shostak, and others. Excessive emphasis on the Kung San has sometimes been criticized by anthropologists. The Kung San are now experiencing the historical crisis in South Africa and thus forced to make decisions that may change their way of life.

# BIBLIOGRAPHY

*A Course in Miracles: Manual for Teachers,* Vol. 3. Tiburon, Calif.: Foundation for Inner Peace, 1975.

Adams, David. "Women Batterers, The Sins of Our Brothers." *Sojourners* (May 1982).

Andrews, Lewis M. *To Thine Own Self Be True.* New York: Doubleday, 1989.

"Are You Addicted to Addiction?" *Utne Reader* (November/December 1988).

Assagioli, Robert. "Synthesis," vols. 1 and 2. Synthesis Press (1975 and 1978).

Bach, Richard. *The Bridge Across Forever.* New York: Morrow, 1984.

Bass, Ellen, and Laura Davis. *The Courage to Heal.* New York: Harper and Row, 1988.

Berne, Eric. *Transactional Analysis in Psychotherapy.* New York: Grove Press, 1961.

——. *What Do You Say after You Say Hello?* New York: Bantam Books, 1972.

Bettelheim, Bruno. *The Uses of Enchantment: The Meaning and Importance of Fairy Tales.* New York: Knopf, 1976.

Bly, Robert. *The Pillow and the Key.* St. Paul: Alley Press, 1987.

——. *Iron John.* Reading, Mass.: Addison-Wesley, 1990.

Briggs, John. An interview of David Bohm, "Quantum Leap." *New Age Journal* (September/October 1989).

Bruchac, Joseph, and Michael Caduto. *Keepers of the Earth.* Golden, Colo.: Fulcrum, 1988.

Campbell, Joseph, and Bill Moyers. *The Power of Myth.* New York: Doubleday, 1988.

Capellanus, Andreas. *The Art of Courtly Love.* Frederick W. Locke, ed. New York: Ungar, 1957.

Capra, Fritjof. *The Turning Point.* New York: Bantam Books, 1983.

——. *Uncommon Wisdom.* New York: Bantam Books, 1989.

Carlson, Richard, and Benjamin Shield. *Healers on Healing.* Los Angeles: Tarcher, 1989.

Castaneda, Carlos. *Journey to Ixtlan.* New York: Simon and Schuster, 1972.

——. *Tales of Power.* New York: Simon and Schuster, 1974.

Chesler, Phyllis, and Emily Jane Goodman. *Women, Money, Power.* New York: Morrow, 1976.

Eagle, White. *The Living Word of St. John.* Marina Del Ray, Calif.: DeVorss, 1979.

Eisler, Riane. *The Chalice and The Blade: Our History, Our Future.* San Francisco: Harper and Row, 1988.

Erskine, Richard G., and Marilyn J. Zalcman. "Rackets and Other Treatment Issues." *Transactional Analysis Journal* 9:1 (January 1979).

Fisher, Helen E. *The Sex Contract: The Evolution of Human Behavior.* New York: Quill, 1983.

Ford, Edward E. *Choosing to Love: A New Way to Respond.* Minneapolis: Winston Press, 1983.

Fox, Matthew. *Original Blessing.* Sante Fe: Bear and Company, 1983.

———. *The Coming of the Cosmic Christ.* San Francisco: Harper and Row, 1988.

French, Marilyn. *Beyond Power.* New York: Ballantine Books, 1986.

Freudenbergh, Herbert J. "Today's Troubled Men." *Psychology Today* (December 1987).

Fromm, Erich. *The Art of Loving.* New York: Harper and Row, 1956.

Gawain, Shakti, and Laurel King. *Living in the Light.* Los Altos, Calif.: New World Library, 1986.

Gibran, Kahlil. *The Prophet.* New York: Alfred A. Knopf, 1969.

Giono, Jean. *The Man Who Planted Trees.* Chelsea, Vt.: Chelsea Green, 1985.

Goulding, Mary McClure, and Robert L. Goulding. *Changing Lives Through Redecision Therapy.* New York: Brunner/Mazel, 1979.

Goulding, Robert, and Mary McClure Goulding. *The Power Is in the Patient.* San Francisco: TA Press, 1978.

Grof, Christina, and Stanislav Grof. *The Stormy Search for the Self.* Los Angeles: Tarcher, 1990.

Grof, Stanislav. *East and West: Ancient Wisdom and Modern Science.* Mill Valley, Calif.: Briggs, Robert, Associates, 1985.

———. *The Adventure of Self Discovery.* Albany, N.Y.: State University of New York Press, 1987.

Groth, A. Nicholas. *Men Who Rape: The Psychology of the Offender.* New York: Plenum Press, 1979.

Hamer, Mike, and Nathaniel Mead. An Interview of Thomas Berry, "Finding Heaven on Earth." *New Age Journal* (April 1990).

Hartshorne, Charles. *The Divine Relativity: A Social Conception of God.* New Haven: Yale University Press, 1948.

Herman, Judith. *Father-Daughter Incest.* Cambridge, Mass.: Harvard University Press, 1981.

House, James S., Karl R. Landis, and Debra Umberson. "Social Relationships and Health." *Science* Vol. 241 (July 1988).

Johnson, Robert. *HE: Understanding Masculine Psychology.* New York: Harper and Row, 1986.

———. *Inner Work.* San Francisco: Harper and Row, 1986.

———. *SHE: Understanding Feminine Psychology.* New York: Harper and Row, 1986.

———. *Ecstasy: Understanding the Psychology of Joy.* San Francisco: Harper and Row, 1989.

Jones, E. Stanley. *The Way to Power and Poise.* Nashville: Abingdon Press, 1949.

Kahler, Taibi. *Transactional Analysis Revisited.* Little Rock: Human Development Publications, 1978.

Kahler, with Hedges Capers. "The Miniscript." *Transactional Analysis Journal* 4:1 (January 1974).

Karpman, Stephen. "Fairy Tales and Script Drama Analysis." *TAB* 7:26 (April 1968).

Keen, Sam. *Beginnings Without End.* San Francisco: Harper and Row, 1977.

Keyes, Ken, Jr. *A Conscious Person's Guide to Relationships.* Coos Bay, Ore.: Love Line Books, 1979.

———. *The Hundreth Monkey.* Coos Bay, Ore.: Vision Books, 1982.

Klein, Carole. *Mother and Sons.* Boston: Houghton Mifflin, 1984.

Konner, Melvin. *The Tangled Wing.* New York: Harper and Row, 1983.

Kupfer, David, and Morris Haimowitz. "Therapeutic Interventions." *Transactional Analysis Journal* 1:1 (1971), 10-16.

Leclerc, Ivor. *Whitehead's Metaphysics.* Lanham, Md.: University Press of America, 1986.

Lerner, Gerda. *The Creation of Patriarchy.* New York: Oxford University Press, 1986.

Levin, Pamela. *Cycles of Power: A User's Guide to the Seven Seasons of Life.* Deerfield Beach, Fla.: Health Communications, 1988.

Lindbergh, Anne Morrow. *Gift from the Sea.* New York: Random House, 1955.

Lovelock, James. *The Ages of Gaia: A Biography of Our Living Earth.* New York: Norton, 1988.

Millman, Dan. *Way of the Peaceful Warrior.* Tiburon, Calif.: H. J. Kramer, 1984.

Mishlove, Jeffrey. "An Interview of Francis Vaughn." *Noetic Sciences Review* No. 10 (Spring 1989).

Neumann, Erich. *The Great Mother.* Princeton, N.J.: Princeton University Press, 1972.

Nordby, Vernon J., and Calvin S. Hall. *A Primer of Jungian Psychology.* New York: Mentor, 1973.

Ode, Kim. "Some Mothers May Not Give Dad a Chance." *Minneapolis Star and Tribune* (January 10, 1988).

Ouspensky, P. D. *In Search of the Miraculous.* New York: Harcourt, Brace, and World, 1949.

———. *The Fourth Way.* New York: Vintage, 1957.

———. *The Psychology of Man's Possible Evolution.* New York: Random House, 1973.

Palmer, Helen. *The Enneagram.* New York: Harper and Row, 1988.

Pearce, Joseph C. *The Bond of Power.* New York: Elseview-Dutton, 1981.

Pearson, Carol S. *The Hero Within.* San Francisco: Harper and Row, 1986.

Peck, M. Scott. *The Road Less Traveled.* New York: Simon and Schuster, 1978.

Rich, Adrienne. *Of Woman Born.* New York: Norton, 1976.

Riso, Don Richard. *Personality Types.* Boston: Houghton Mifflin, 1987.

———. *Understanding the Enneagram.* Boston: Houghton Mifflin, 1990.

Robertson, James. *The Sane Alternative: A Choice of Futures.* St. Paul: River Basin, 1978.

Schaef, Anne Wilson. *When Society Becomes an Addict.* San Francisco: Harper and Row, 1987.

Schaeffer, Brenda. *Corrective Parenting Chart*, 3rd ed. Brenda Schaeffer: Minneapolis, 1981.

——. *Is It Love or Is It Addiction?* Center City, Minn.: Hazelden Educational Materials, 1987.

Schiff, J. L., et al. *The Cathexis Reader.* New York: Harper and Row, 1975.

Shinn, Florence Scovel. *The Game of Life and How to Play It.* Marina Del Ray, Calif.: DeVorss, 1978.

Sinetar, Marsha. *Ordinary People as Monks and Mystics.* Mahwah, N.J.: Paulist Press, 1986.

Small, Jacquelyn. *Transformers—The Therapists of the Future.* Marina del Ray, Calif.: DeVorss, 1982.

Steiner, Claude M. *Scripts People Live.* New York: Grove, 1974.

Steinsaltz, Adin. *The Thirteen Petalled Rose.* New York: Basic Books, 1980.

Stoltz, Sandra Gordon. *The Food Fix.* Englewood Cliffs, N.J.: Prentice-Hall, 1983.

Suchocki, Marjorie Hewitt. *God-Christ-Church: A Practical Approach to Process Theology.* New York: Crossroad, 1982.

Tart, Charles T. *Transpersonal Psychologies.* New York: Harper and Row, 1975.

Teresa, Mother. *Words to Love By. . . .* Notre Dame, Ind.: Ave Marie Press, 1983.

Trungpa, Chogyam. *Shambhala: The Sacred Path of the Warrior.* New York: Bantam Books, 1986.

Wallis, Claudia, "Back Off Buddy." *Time* (October 12, 1987).

Weed, Joseph J. *Wisdom of the Mystic Masters.* West Nyack, N.Y.: Parker, 1968.

Weiss, Laurie, and Jonathan Weiss. *Recovery from Co-Dependency.* Deerfield Beach, Fla.: Health Communications, 1989.

Wilber, Ken. *No Boundary: Eastern and Western Approaches to Personal Growth.* Boston: Shambhala, 1979.

——. "Love Story." *New Age Journal* (July/August 1989).

——. ed. *The Holographic Paradigm and Other Paradoxes.* Boulder, Colo.: Shambhala, 1982.

Wilhelm, Richard. *The I Ching or Book of Changes.* Cary F. Baynes, trans. Princeton, N.J.: Princeton University Press, 1977.

# INDEX